The Benefits
of the
New Economy

RESOLVING THE GLOBAL ECONOMIC CRISIS
THROUGH MUTUAL GUARANTEE

The Benefits
of the
New Economy

RESOLVING THE GLOBAL ECONOMIC CRISIS
THROUGH MUTUAL GUARANTEE

The ARI Institute Department of Economics

THE BENEFITS OF THE NEW ECONOMY
Resolving the global economic crisis through mutual guarantee

Copyright © 2012 by MICHAEL LAITMAN
All rights reserved
Published by ARI Publishers
www.ariresearch.org   info@ariresearch.org
1057 Steeles Avenue West, Suite 532, Toronto, ON, M2R 3X1, Canada
2009 85th Street #51, Brooklyn, New York, 11214, USA

Printed in Canada

Library of Congress Control Number: 2012936508

ISBN: 978-1-897448-73-1

Authors: Guy Isaac, Joseph Levy, Alexander Ognits
Content Editors: Michael Kor, Shlomi Bohana
Translation: Chaim Ratz
Associate Editor: Mary Miesem
Copy Editor: Claire Gerus
Layout: Baruch Khovov
Cover: Inna Smirnova
Executive Editor: Chaim Ratz
Publishing and Post Production: Uri Laitman

FIRST EDITION: JANUARY 2013
FIRST PRINTING

CONTENTS

APPENDICES

A GLOBAL-INTEGRAL WORLD

Globalization: "Globalization" refers to the increasingly international relationships involving culture, people, and economic activity. Most often it refers to economics: the planetary distribution of locations where goods and services are produced, enabled through the reduction of barriers to international trade such as tariffs, export fees, and import quotas. Globalization has accompanied and contributed to economic growth in developed and developing countries through increased specialization and the principle of comparative advantage (the ability of a person or a country to produce a particular good or service at a lower cost). The term can also refer to the transnational circulation of ideas, languages, and popular culture.

Integral: entire, complete, whole. Also, consisting or composed of parts that together constitute a whole.

Foreword

Two issues mark 2011 as a turning point in history. The first is the worldwide social unrest, and the second is the global economic crisis.

The social unrest began with "the Arab Spring," an uprising that led to the fall of regimes in Egypt and Libya, and chaos and bloodshed in Syria. Social unrest quickly spread to Europe, with tent-cities appearing in Spain, riots in Greece and the U.K., and various forms of civil protest in several other countries. Finally, protest arrived in the U.S. with the "occupy movement" that began in New York City and spread like bushfire throughout the country.

This global unrest had a common root—the sense that social injustice was being perpetrated. Finally, people rose up, determined that their voices would no longer be ignored; they demanded that economic sufficiency and democracy, in the case of the Arab Spring, would be given to all. In Europe and in the U.S., another demand was put on the table—to narrow the gap between the wealthiest 1% of the population and the other 99%, and to change, or at least mend the capitalist system that has allowed such gaps to be created.

The second major issue was the global economic crisis. The tools that decision-makers used, such as cutting interest rates, pouring torrents of money into the market, or establishing aid funds, had become utterly inefficient as the global economy continued its downward spiral. The world stopped behaving the way economists had predicted it would because the world had changed since the paradigms of classical economics were laid out. Unfortunately, economists had not changed their paradigms accordingly. The new world is a global-integral one, where every event, whether a natural disaster or a global crisis, affects the entire world. The interdependence among all elements of the global system is a fact that must be taken into account, as both the debt crisis in Europe and the earthquake in Japan clearly demonstrate.

The social unrest and the global economic crisis are closely linked. As the same groups carried out protests against both the economic system and social injustices, it became clear that economy and society are interlinked. In fact, our economy *reflects* the nature of our society, the way we relate to one another.

The expansion of global trade and technological advancement helped tighten our connections even more, transcending borders, culture, religion, and race. The world has now become a small village, where anyone is one free internet call away from anyone else.

And yet, the economic paradigm that we have been following for decades has become obsolete. Worse yet, its premises of free competition and maximizing personal gain, founded on the belief that those traits would keep the system healthy and running, have proven themselves wrong. We have made consumption a culture we call "consumerism," we have consecrated and venerated individualism and entitlement, and we have created inequality so extreme that 1% of the world population possesses 40% of the world's wealth! The rest of the world suffers from deepening financial insecurity, or worse. Even in the most developed countries, millions go to bed hungry each night, tens of millions have no health insurance, and millions are not only indigent, but hopeless.

The Earth can provide abundantly for all of us, but our mutual alienation prevents us from distributing food and other necessities to those in need. The global crisis and global protests testify that people are no longer willing to tolerate this injustice, and that transformation has become the call of the hour.

The first thing to change must be human relations; after all, that is the root of the problem. When that element has changed, the rest of life's systems will change accordingly. In a global-integral world where all are interdependent, the prevailing spirit of human relations should be one of mutual guarantee, where all are guarantors of each other's well-being.

If we ponder the meaning of the network of connections we have formed through globalization, we will see that the incongruity between our self-centered approach and the interdependent nature of our connections is the cause of the crisis. And since globalization is an irreversible fact of life, what's left is for us to adjust our relations to this reality. Therefore, if we assume a *modus operandi* of mutual guarantee—which is congruent with interdependence—we will resolve both the global crisis and social unrest.

This book contains thirteen "stand-alone" essays written in 2011 by several economists and financiers from different disciplines. Each essay addresses a specific issue and can be read as a separate unit, but one *leitmotif* connects them—the absence of mutual guarantee as the cause of our problems in the global-integral world.

You can read the essays in the order of your choice. We, the authors, believe that if you read at least several of the essays, you will form a more inclusive picture of the shift suggested in the pages ahead, the transformation required to resolve the global crisis and create a sustainable, prosperous economy.

To facilitate the shift as quickly and smoothly as possible, the influence of the environment is key. The key to a successful transition from independent to interdependent paradigm lies in expansive education and circulation of a) the necessity to change, b) the nature of the required change. The media and the education system can and should play a lead role in creating an environment that both informs people of the kind of change required, and supports its expansion.

A solution must not be forced. This will only lead to a painful failure. To achieve mutual guarantee, we must mutually take part in rebuilding our social values. This should be done within the framework of a social-economic treaty, and it should unfold gradually, maintaining broad consensus and deliberation throughout the process. If we work in this way, we believe that the global crisis will manifest as a golden opportunity for all of humanity. It will enable us to live in lasting economic and financial security, based on a connection of mutual guarantee among all people. The change must, of course, begin with us.

THE ECONOMY AS A REFLECTION OF HUMAN RELATIONS

A TRUE AND LASTING ECONOMIC IMPROVEMENT DEPENDS ON CHANGING HUMAN RELATIONS

Key Points

- The economy is a reflection of our social relations. Hence, the crisis in the economy is first and foremost a crisis in our interrelations.
- The function of man is egoistic—aiming to maximize profit for self. In a reality of scarcity, that function creates an inherent conflict between people, manifesting in competition and a zero-sum game where one's gain is necessarily another's loss.
- There is interdependence among us in the global-integral world into which humanity has evolved. This is why the egoistic connections among us have stopped functioning.

That gap between our egoism and our interconnectedness is the reason for the crisis.

- The laws of the global-integral world compel us to connect in mutual guarantee and act as cells in a single organism for the benefit of the entire populace.
- When mutual guarantee and social solidarity are the basis of a new economic paradigm—a balanced and functional economy—as dictated by the laws of the global-integral world, we will achieve a life of comfort, personal and social prosperity, and a harmonious and sustainable system.
- Providing information and education, and creating a supportive environment are necessary for us to connect in mutual guarantee.

THE GLOBAL ECONOMIC CRISIS
IS CHALLENGING THE ECONOMIC PARADIGM

According to classic economics, people aspire to maximize profits for completely egoistic motives. The 17th century British philosopher, Thomas Hobbes, put it this way: "Every man is presumed to seek what is good for himself naturally, and what is just, only for peace's sake, and accidentally."[1] That view, which is still prevalent, asserts that social behavior is merely an after-the-fact result, and that our forefathers made social treaties only for the profits they yielded, not because they were drawn to each other's company.

In the last decade, a new school of thought has emerged, known as "behavioral economics." This new school focuses on the actual human behavior, rather than on abstract market forces, and regards that behavior as a means to understand the way we make financial decisions. Behavioral economics describes the nature and power of human relations, their collaborations, and

---

1   Thomas Hobbes, *Rudiments*, 1651, iii

the extent to which tendencies and fundamental perceptions of human economics rely on values of mutuality.

The current global crisis and our unsuccessful attempts to solve it could mean that the answers to humanity's challenges lie in those new avenues of research. Indeed, thus far every attempt to resolve the crisis has failed. Interest rate cuts, bailouts, expansion programs, and increasing government deficits are based on classical economics, which rely on a collection of monetary moves (primarily interest rate cuts) and fiscal steps (expanding government budgets, tax cuts and so forth).

Government intervention and central bank assistance was meant to nudge the market back into balance. The subsequent failure to achieve this suggests that it is time to replace the existing economic paradigm. Any new paradigm must rise one level higher and show that the problem and hence the solution are at the level of human relations rather than the monetary level.

BEHAVIORAL ECONOMICS IMPLIES A NEW DIRECTION AND A NEW SOLUTION TO THE CRISIS

If we understand the critical impact that the nature of people's relations has on the economy, we will understand the kind of economic system that we must build in order for it to carry out its roles effectively and maintain its stability. When the economic and financial systems adapt themselves to the global-integral world, where economic ties cross borders and firms, and where people depend on and affect one another, it will stabilize the socioeconomic system. Only then will the system avoid shocks and frequent crises that take a heavy toll on us. Previous solutions to these crises are inadequate, which is why at the start of 2012 the world is facing a severe economic situation, which is actually a continuation of the crisis that began in the summer of 2007.

Yet, not only the economy must change. Because the economic and financial systems are reflections of human relations, the entire international community must provide solutions that rearrange the system of human relations. In other words, when our attitudes change toward bonding, unity, social cohesion, care for others, and mutual guarantee, we will discover the solution to today's economic paradigm..

The Evolution of the Economy

People cannot exist without regard to society. As social beings, we are compelled to live among people, be assisted by them, and contribute our share for the common good. The evolution of humanity from the clan of the caveman through feudalism and onto capitalism reflects the evolution of our interconnections and our interdependence. In accord with those changes, the way we trade and exchange goods and services has also evolved to reflect the times and their characteristics.

In prehistoric times, humans lived in clans. Then came villages, then cities, and then states. For tens of thousands of years, people worked to provide for themselves, their kin, and the people near them. But as international trade evolved, developed nations began to conquer undeveloped ones and discover new lands. The industrial revolution prompted urbanization and tightened the connections among people.

Commerce and Exchange

It is through commerce and exchange that today's economy has evolved. This economy is driven by humankind's egoism, which strives to profit, even at the expense of others. One person may be a farmer, another may be a manufacturer, and by connecting, they both benefit. This is why we have built all our connections in parity with our egoistic nature. In the past, it involved the exchange of products without the use of money. Later, we learned to use coins of precious metals, and then paper notes that represented the financial value of the one who issued them.

Today the majority of money transfers are actually virtual. The transfer is made from one account to another via computer networks. The Information Technology Revolution has dramatically changed human relations, and the virtualization of relations is expressed through finance and money markets, as well.

It follows that the economy is a type of compromise between individual egos and the necessity to connect in order to be sustained by one another, by some sort of general consent. Clearly, the global economy has much to do with power games and politics, as well as with moral considerations, that are not taken into account in the paradigm of classical economics.

Instead, economics deals with contrasting elements and is not subject to the physical laws of Nature. Rather, it is our own creation, expressing one means we use to survive as a species, and how we approach certain relationships. This is of paramount importance, because instead of trying to force an outdated paradigm on ourselves, we could fashion a different one that expresses the change in human interaction that exists in today's interconnected world, in the interdependence and reciprocity of economic and social ties, which are only tightening.

THE WHOLE TRUTH ABOUT THE ECONOMIC CRISIS

This crisis is expressed in our approach to the world and to society. The crisis is within us and in our interrelations. Nature works in harmony and balance, and now it is up to us to change ourselves and how we relate to others. As a result, the systems we have built, including the socioeconomic system, must be balanced and harmonious, as is Nature.

Among the characteristics of the economic crisis are bloated prices of products, services, stocks, and loans. As a result, we are witnessing a crisis of trust in the economy. At the end of the day, the false picture of the world that was built and cultivated for many years by those with their own agendas has disintegrated. People have begun to understand that in an economy based on lies, speculation, and manipulation it is impossible to trust anyone. Not surprisingly, in a state of general mistrust, today's economic system is unsustainable.

Thus, our contemporary economy is a snapshot of a world of distorted interconnections, manipulations, and false values. Unscrupulous and unrestrained competition has been created, along with irrational consumer behavior, as consumers falsely believe that what they buy defines their essence ("I buy, therefore I am"). Today, society's values are determined by brand names, celebrities, and status symbols, not by people's rational interests. Under these circumstances, the economy's collapse was only a matter of time.

THE GAP BETWEEN A WORLD-TURNED-GLOBAL AND THE ANACHRONISTIC ECONOMY

A more systemic explanation of the root of the crisis is that the world has become global and connected. Every system, including economic and social, is linked to another, affects one another, and is affected by one another. The money markets, for instance, are a single global system. Therefore, whatever happens in the U.S. affects Europe and the rest of the world, and vice-versa. The stock markets have long become a global barometer that expresses our hopes, our despair, our crises, and our growth.

Also, money markets are affecting other systems, especially the business world, the performance of economies, and our personal financial well-being. The world has become a complex global system of interdependent systems, connected in a way that we did not choose, but which we cannot ignore.

At the same time, however, our human relations are still based on individualistic values. Our relations are inherently self-centered and competitive, and have changed very little in the past several centuries. Naturally, since our economy reflects those relationships, it also reflects those values.

We are facing a huge gap between the laws of the global-integral world, and the egoistic nature of human relations and the economy derived from them. That gap is the real reason we are experiencing economic and social crises. Until we bridge that gap, we will continue to experience this gap as a crisis.

The laws of the new world compel us to bond and to change the economic and social systems to become based on mutual consideration, cooperation, and synergy, on sharing of resources and knowledge, on balanced consumption, and unification of economic, monetary, and fiscal mechanisms. Both these systems express the mutual guarantee among people, while the current economy continues to be based on maximizing benefit and personal gain and competition, and thus supports an inherent conflict among people.

Due to the importance of money in our lives, the economic crisis is receiving much attention, and the economic dependence among countries and stock markets is clear and accepted by all. Yet a similar interdependence exists in other systems, such as ecology, education, and science. In fact, every system affected by human relations is now in crisis.

CRISIS AS AN OPPORTUNITY

By and large, the rise of a new economic system has taken humanity by surprise. In the past, we built connections and social and economic systems to match our needs and the way in which we interrelate. Now, suddenly, these systems seem insufficient to manage our lives so we can live in peace and comfort. Instead, the global-integral system seems to have its own laws.

The interdependence and tightening connections among all of life's systems leave us no choice but to change our own interconnections accordingly. Interdependence among people, firms, and countries cannot exist in an economic system based on a zero-sum game, characterized by aggressive competition, an emphasis on maximizing personal gain, and manipulation.

The interdependence among the various elements of the global system is in stark contrast to the social and economic gaps that continue to exist within and between countries. This global, ego-based system has become completely ineffective, making it impossible to continue using it. Indeed, the relationships we built previously have led to this crisis. In a sense, the crisis offers us an opportunity to examine the nature of our relations and to change it so it fits what is required in this global world, and the necessary interdependence of its parts. Such harmony and congruence will necessarily create a different economy, this one more optimistic, balanced, and stable.

ECONOMY AND HUMAN RELATIONS

At the end of the day, the network of connections between us determines everything. That network is spread out throughout the world, and consists of many elements—countries, armies, funds, raw materials, religious denominations, social ties, hopes for the future, and so forth. All are parts of that network among us, which is why that concept is so difficult for us to grasp.. For now, those who can grasp it are those profiting most from it.

Many people argue that we should examine the financial system and correct it. But we need to understand that the whole of reality has changed. The system has become global and integral, and this is what hinders our attempts to live with the current socioeconomic system. Everything we built in the existing system stemmed from our egoistic nature. But our current reality necessitates that we reciprocate rather than exploit. The connection between us is much tighter now and compels us to "upgrade" our connections toward unity and mutual guarantee (in which all are guarantors of each other's well-being).

Because we don't know how to approach the global-integral network, we are losing our ability to properly communicate with others. This is why we face this worldwide crisis in trust. The banks don't believe the manufacturers, citizens don't believe their governments, and the governments don't believe each other.

In the past, communication was clear and relied on give and take, on individual consideration of profit and loss, and on the necessity to cooperate, even if against our will. The ego played a key role and we all understood that this was so.

In the global-integral system of connections, however, we need an economy that reflects the interdependence among us, but we haven't adapted our "operating system" to it. We are still living in economic and social systems based on how we handled relationships in the past.

At the same time, we are discovering the interdependence among us. The problem is that we have yet to understand how this works. We have not even detected its altruistic nature! Here lies the problem: this contemporary crisis cannot be resolved in the old ways, since everything depends on how quickly humanity can bond and move towards mutual guarantee.

Economists Are at a Loss

The toolbox of classical economics is inadequate for our time, and our antiquated thinking is driving us even deeper into the current crisis. Clearly, this must be changed, as Joseph Stiglitz, Nobel Prize laureate in economics, said in a lecture at the 4th Meeting of Economic Sciences at Lindau, "The standard macroeconomic models have failed by all the most important tests of scientific theory. They did not predict that the financial crisis would happen; and when it did, they understated its effects."[2]

2   "Short films from the 2011 Lindau Nobel Laureate Meeting in Economic Sciences," *The New Palgrave Dictionary of Economics Online,* http://www.dictionaryofeconomics.com/ resources/news_lindau_meeting

We need to adapt ourselves and the nature of our relations to the qualities of our connections in the global-integral system. By continuing to develop behavioral economics, we are taking a step in the right direction—just as the economy has become global, so have our social relations. This is why ego-based relations do not work anymore. We must learn the qualities required of relationships in the new world. This will not only bring us into balance with the global-integral world, but will enable us to understand and welcome the changes that social and economic systems must undergo.

The change is inevitable; it cannot be stopped. The more we deny it, the more we will experience the change as a crisis. But if instead we come to grasp the meaning of the change and make the necessary changes, feelings of distress will give way to hope and prosperity, and to harmony and peace, both among each other and between humanity and Nature.

Therefore, all that needs to change is the nature of our interrelations. If we commit to a new social and economic treaty, a global and integral one, with mutual guarantee among us, we will be able to begin transforming the existing economic paradigm, and that of every system of life humanity has built. Such a change is possible only through broad education and information. This will create an empathetic environment that nurtures the values of mutual guarantee and stresses its advantages. Only such an evolutionary process will guarantee a stable, efficient economy that provides harmonious, balanced, and sustainable living for all.

A Global-Integral World
Requires a New Economy

THE CURRENT ECONOMIC METHOD
CANNOT CONTINUE TO EXIST
IN A GLOBAL-INTEGRAL WORLD

Key Points

- When every country is connected by trade and financial ties, irrevocable interdependence is created.
- The global crisis has exposed the extent to which the fate of all counties is linked to each other in a global-integral world. Solutions that relate to only one country are inapplicable, and resolving this global crisis is possible only through a systemic solution that takes into account the interdependence among countries.
- Every measure taken by world leaders to resolve the crisis has failed and bewilderment regarding the proper means of action prevails.

- The key to resolving the crisis is in closing the gaps between the laws of the global-integral world and the self-centered, competitive economy. It is vital to adapt the economic systems to the principle of mutual guarantee, in which all are guarantors of each other's well-being.
- It is imperative to provide information and education and to create a supportive environment so we can connect in mutual guarantee.

THE ENORMOUS SCOPE OF GLOBAL TRADE CREATES MUTUAL DEPENDENCE

International trade has been part of the economy since ancient times. The means of trading improve along with technology, and along with them evolves the international trading.

In the past, countries could close themselves in an autarkic market, existing within a self-sufficient economy that does not rely on trade with other countries. Today, however, this is not possible. There is not a country in the world that does not export or import goods and services. In fact, there is not a country in the world that can provide for all the needs of its citizens on its own ignoring the international system.

According to data from the World Trade Organization (WTO), since WWII, the scope of international trade has risen sharply. The United States was the leader in international merchandise trade in 2010, with a trade volume of 3.25 trillion dollars (1.97 of which is imports); China was second, with approximately 2.97 trillion dollars in volume (with 183 billion dollars in merchandise trade surplus), and Germany was third with 2.34 trillion in merchandise trade volume (with a surplus of 202 billion dollars).[3]

---

3   "International Trade Statistics 2011," *World Trade Organization*, www.wto.org/english/res_e/statis_e/its2011_e/its2011_e.pdf

The enormous scope of international trade exemplifies the connections and dependence among the countries, both in the real economy[4] and in finance.

MUTUAL TIES AND CONNECTIONS IN PRODUCTION OF GOODS AND SERVICES (REAL ECONOMY)

In the real economy, there are diverse economic ties that manifest in trade of goods and services. One such example is the trade connections in the auto industry between Japan and the United States. The earthquake that struck Japan on March 11, 2011 had a major impact on the U.S. car industry because it stalled production lines and the importation of spare parts, and diminished the imports of cars from Japan to the U.S.

Following the rise in the price of cars, car sales dropped, which led to a reduction in Personal Consumption Expenditure (PCE), and hence in the performance of the U.S. economy as a whole.

THE FINANCIAL SYSTEM—A MIRROR OF THE GLOBAL WORLD

As in real economy, profound interdependence has evolved in the financial sector, as well, whether through loans (bonds) that countries took from other countries or through other means. The most conspicuous example of that interdependence is the massive amounts of U.S bonds held by the Chinese government. Because of the speed at which money markets respond to changes in the policies and in the economy, these markets have become the most prominent characteristic of the global and interconnected world we live in. The interdependence among countries and investors is palpable and tangible in those markets.

Another distinct example is the sovereign debt crisis, which is currently unfolding in the Eurozone countries. The enormous

---

4   Real Economy: The part of the economy that is concerned with actually producing goods and services, as opposed to the part of the economy that is concerned with buying and selling on the financial markets. Source: Financial Times Lexicon (http://lexicon.ft.com/Term?term=real-economy)

debt of many countries demonstrates how all are in the same boat. The United States owes trillion dollars to Eurozone countries and to Japan, and trillions more to China, Russia, and many other owners of U.S. bonds. Germany owes 5.46 trillion dollars to the above-mentioned countries; the PIIGS countries (Portugal, Ireland, Italy, Greece, and Spain) owe a total of 6.4 trillion dollars to those countries, and France owes them 5.46 trillion dollars.[5]

The economic and financial ties compel countries to become more involved in each other's internal affairs out of fear for their own economies. On the one hand, financial interdependence accelerates international efforts to aid troubled countries, both directly and through the International Monetary Fund (IMF). On the other hand, financial and/or political interference could be construed as a threat to the country's sovereignty and may instigate tension and conflict.

In regard to the crisis in the American economy, Chinese officials criticized the United States for its colossal budget deficit, which could undermine the stability of the U.S. economy and its ability to repay its debt to China and to other debt-holders. The tension wrought by the criticism prompted Chinese Vice President, Xi Jinping, to state, "The US economy is always highly resilient and has a strong self-repair capacity. We believe the US economy will achieve better development in the process of coping with challenges."[6]

Because approximately half of U.S. bonds are purchased by foreign investors, primarily China, Japan, Russia, and India, the international monetary system's sensitivity to the American economy and to the U.S. government treatment of it is obvious. A comment that demonstrates the involvement among countries was made by the U.S. Treasury Secretary, Timothy Geithner.

---

5   "Eurozone debt web: Who owes what to whom?," *BBC News Business* (November 18, 2011), http://www.bbc.co.uk/news/business-15748696
6   "Xi Jinping and US Vice President Biden Attend China-US Business Dialogue," *Ministry of Foreign Affairs of the People's Republic of China*, (August 19, 2011), http://www.fmprc.gov.cn/eng/zxxx/t850833.htm

In an official statement to the IMF, Geithner said, in regard to Europe, "The threat of cascading default, bank runs, and catastrophic risk must be taken off the table, as otherwise it will undermine all other efforts, both within Europe and globally. ...Decisions as to how to conclusively address the region's problems cannot wait until the crisis gets more severe."[7]

THE TIGHTENING ECONOMIC AND FINANCIAL TIES AMONG COUNTIES

International trade began as a means to provide for a country's needs. As capitalism spread throughout the world, the primary motive of countries changed from provision of necessities to maximizing their profits to maintain a strong, stable economy, and allow for continued development of their economies and their citizens' well-being. The global balance was formed through international demand and supply on both economic and financial levels.

In the real economy, the efficiency of production in some countries, and the differences in production costs can lead them to export their products to other countries that have a demand for that product. On the financial level, each country strives to profit on its currency and hence lends to others. Yet, because the country needs money to keep up with government and public expenses, and to keep investing to create meaningful growth, it will also borrow from other countries.

Countries also diversify their investments among different countries to diminish the risk and to build a secure investment portfolio. Their wish to maximize their profits compels them to keep up with developments in industry, technology, and finance in other countries. Doing so has strengthened trade, as well as political connections among countries and throughout the global economic system. This is how the world has become irrevocably global and integral.

---

7   Ben Rooney, "Geithner sounds alarm on Europe," *CNN Money*, (September 25, 2011), http://money.cnn.com/2011/09/24/markets/geithner_debt/index.htm

THE HELPLESSNESS OF ECONOMISTS
AND DECISION MAKERS

The interdependence among countries was one of the key reasons for the expansion of the crisis from the United States to the international economy in 2008. Now, as in 2008, every country is affected by the crisis. The complex links among countries and corporations require integrated moves among countries, as well as mutual consideration and genuine willingness to support faltering economies. It seems that the message, "we're all in the same boat" has indeed sunk in. Yet, attempts to resolve the crisis through monetary or financial stimuli have failed bitterly in both the U.S. and Europe.

The world's inability to deal with the roots of the global crisis since 2008 perplexes our economists and decision-makers. They ponder how to conduct trade and use the vast financial system in a world turned global and integral, as well as how to manage countries' desire to maximize their profits separately, using economic reciprocity. The gap between the mandatory reciprocity imposed by the interdependence among countries in the global-integral world, and the current nature of the international economic system—based on narrow and self-centered approaches—is now recognized by the international economic community as a crisis.

Nouriel Roubini, Professor of Economics at New York University and one of the few who predicted the global credit crisis back in 2004, stated in the summer of 2011 regarding the escalating global crisis, "Karl Marx had it right. At some point, capitalism can self-destroy itself."[8] Likewise, Nobel Prize winner

---

8   Nouriel Roubini Blog, http://nourielroubiniblog.blogspot.com/2011/10/karl-marx-had-it-right.html (originally said in a video recording to the WSJ: http://online.wsj.com/video/roubini-warns-of-global-recession-risk/C036B113-6D5F-4524-A5AF-DF2F3E2F8735.html)

Joseph Stiglitz,, stated, "In a way, not only is there a crisis in our economy, there ought to be a crisis in economics."[9]

Also, in September 13, 2011, Mohamed A. El-Erian, CEO and co-founder of PIMCO, the largest investment firm and bond fund in the world, stated in a radio interview on "Bloomberg Surveillance" with Tom Keene and Ken Prewitt, "We're getting close to a full-blown banking crisis in Europe. ... We are in a synchronized global slowdown. There's very little confidence in economic policy making both in Europe and the U.S.."[10]

On a different occasion, Mr. El-Erian, "Gave four reasons constraining an improvement in the global economy. Oil prices ... are too elevated, housing markets haven't sufficiently stabilized, Europe hasn't solved its debt crisis, and world leaders are concerned that U.S. politicians are 'arguing too much.' Different sections of the orchestra are playing a different tune and it sounds confusing."[11]

These statements and others by leading economists and financiers demonstrate how countries' aspirations to maximize their profits have led them to interdependence. At the same time, these statements testify to their bewilderment and inability to cope with the global economic reality.

Is GLOBAL INTEGRATION AN UNAVOIDABLE FACT?

Along with the integration required in light of the above-described economic connections, China, the second most powerful economy in the world, recently stated that it intends to stall its investment policy in Europe and the United States.

9   "Short films from the 2011 Lindau Nobel Laureate Meeting in Economic Sciences," *The New Palgrave Dictionary of Economics Online*, http://www.dictionaryofeconomics.com/ resources/news_lindau_meeting (the above-mentioned statement is in Stiglitz's video after 10:05 minutes.

10   John Detrixhe and Tom Keene, "Europe Close to Banking Crisis, El-Erian Says: Tom Keene," *Bloomberg* (September 13, 2011), http://www.bloomberg.com/news/2011-09-13/ europe-close-to-banking-crisis-el-erian.html

11   Jason Kelly and Laura Marcinek, "Pimco's El-Erian Says U.S. Unemployment Is 'Stubbornly High,'" *Business Week* (May 2, 2011), http://www.businessweek.com/ news/2011-05-02/pimco-s-el-erian-says-u-s-unemployment-is-stubbornly-high-.html

Wen Jiabao, Prime Minister of China, said in an address at the Annual Meeting of the New Champions 2011, "Governments should fulfill their responsibilities and put their own house in order. The major developed economies should adopt responsible and effective fiscal and monetary policies, properly handle debt issues."[12] Additionally, the Bank of China froze foreign currency deals with several major European banks, including Société Générale, Crédit Agricole, and BNP Paribas, in light of the debt crisis in Europe and Moody's credit rating downgrades of several major banks in Europe.

Japan expressed a similar view in a statement by the Japanese Finance Minister, Jun Azumi, in a G20 finance ministers and central bankers meeting in Paris October of 2011, "Europe needs to get its act together because unless the crisis is put to an end, it will start to affect emerging economies which have enjoyed strong growth."[13]

The attitudes of China and Japan to the debt crisis in Europe raise the questions, "Is the isolationistic tendency of China and Japan feasible in today's global and integral world? Can protectionism and separatism of powers maintain their economic stability? Can they disconnect their relations with other nations and become self-sufficient?"

The answer to all the above is a resounding "no." The days when a country could single-handedly provide for all its needs are gone and will not return. In the global-integral world, even the most powerful economies depend on one another and on the entire international system (perhaps more than all the others). Thus, a slowdown in the U.S. economy will induce a sharp decline in China's and Japan's exports and will hurt those countries' economies.

---

12   http://www.gov.cn/english/2011-09/14/content_1947644_5.htm
13   "G20 nations urge Europe to act decisively on debt," *Reuters* (October 15, 2011), http://www.france24.com/en/20111015-debt-crisis-europe-us-g20-pledges-adequate-funding-for-imf

Additionally, government bond markets have become a global arena where countries raise funds from other countries and invest their own reserves in bonds of other countries. Imagine what would happen to the Chinese economy, now one of the two greatest bondholders of U.S. government bonds, if America were unable to repay its debt or declared a debt-restructuring arrangement.

EFFORTS TO OVERCOME THE GLOBAL CRISIS HAVE BEEN A FAILURE

Since the global crisis that began in 2008, the United States and the Eurozone countries have been trying to save their economies from collapse using various bailouts and emergency plans. By and large, these programs rely on monetary expansion, primarily using interest rate cuts and fiscal expansion, which means pouring government funds into the economic system and offering tax benefits to resuscitate the economic activity.

The botchy stimulus policy of the United States government included three stimulus programs of unprecedented magnitude.[14] Yet, Charles I. Plosser, the Philadelphia Fed President, said in that regard, "The notion persists that activist monetary policy can help stabilize the macro-economy... In my view, monetary policy's ability to neutralize the real economic consequences of such shocks is actually quite limited ... Attempts to stabilize the economy will, more likely than not, end up providing stimulus when none is needed, or vice versa. ...So asking monetary policy to do what it cannot do with aggressive attempts at stabilization can actually increase economic instability rather than reduce it."[15]

Marc Faber, a renowned economist and the author of the "Gloom, Boom and Doom" report, was slightly more direct

---

14   Described in the chapter, "Mutual Guarantee as a Practical Solution," section "The Failed 'Practical' Steps in the United States."
15   James Saft, "Don't expect coordinated easing," *Reuters* (September 22, 2011),http://blogs.reuters.com/james-saft/tag/federal-reserve/

in his response to the aforementioned plan. He described the package as "Another complete failure of Keynesian economics and corrupt interventions," Dr. Faber summed up his words about the program, calling it "A complete joke."[16]

As in the United States, the Eurozone countries took several steps that included pumping funds into their markets and cutting interest rates of central banks in Europe. Also, the Eurozone established a European rescue fund with hundreds of billions in Euros for the more vulnerable countries in the bloc.

The IMF also contributed its share in assisting Europe, allocating many billions in bailout money. Many countries in Europe are now carrying out austerity measures to reduce the deficit and to meet the criteria for receiving aid from the rescue funds. However, the budget cuts hurt countries' abilities to revive their economies and to help their citizens. This made matters even worse, causing millions to go out and demonstrate in Greece, Spain, Portugal, and other countries in Europe.

The failure of the incentive policies of the United States and the Eurozone countries set the stage for a crisis in 2011 that dwarfed the one that began a few years earlier. Treating problems on a local level not only failed to resolve problems, it even aggravated them, with the great debts moving from banks and financial institutions into state budgets.

Christine Lagarde, head of the IMF, said "The spectrum of policies available to the various governments and central banks is narrower because a lot of the ammunition was used in 2009."[17] Prof. Roubini said in that regard, "We have reached a stall speed in the economy, not just in the U.S., but also in the

---

16   Patrick Allen, "Marc Faber: Obama's Job Package 'a Complete Joke,'" *CNBC* (September 9, 2011), http://www.cnbc.com/id/44449276/Marc_Faber_Obama_s_Job_Package_a_Complete_Joke

17   "There Has Been a Clear Crisis of Confidence," *Spiegel Online International* (April 9, 2011), http://www.spiegel.de/international/world/0,1518,784115,00.html

Eurozone and the U.K.. ...Unfortunately, we are running out of policy tools."[18]

THE RECIPE FOR RESOLVING THE CRISIS

The global ties among countries is a done deal, a result of natural evolution that is still continuing. In fact, the ties are only strengthening, and the crisis in 2008 clearly exposed that single network in which the fates of all countries are interlinked.

In 2008, the network tried to revive itself through local treatment of the most conspicuous symptoms of the crisis. Moreover, it tried to do it in unprecedented proportions.

However, the international system is following economic, social, and political paradigms that were fashioned after WWII and are no longer suitable for today's global network of economic and social ties. Now, a binding mutual responsibility has been formed among all the countries, and the discrepancy between the nature of the economic global system—and the anachronistic modus operandi that reflect values of economic independence at all cost, maximizing profits and gains, and unrestrained competition—is at the heart of the global crisis.

Decision-makers and economists the world over failed to adopt a broader perspective on the global reality, by which the connections among countries obligate them to develop ties of mutual guarantee among them, if not willingly, then because the facts of life demand it. In the global-integral world of connections of trade, economy, banking, and finance, a country that is concerned with only its own economy, irrespective of the rest of the countries, will fail utterly, damaging the entire international system, which strives for balance, harmony, and collaboration, as it should be when its parts are all interdependent. Even if the economy of such a rogue country should strive, it will inevitably

---

18   "Roubini on U.S. Recession Risk, Europe and China," *Bloomberg* (August 31, 2011), http://www.bloomberg.com/video/74655083/

be affected by the crises in weaker economies, as is the case with Germany in the 2011 Eurozone debt crisis.

Thus, devising a solution requires a comprehensive, global move, with cooperation and mutual guarantee among the countries. This will manifest in mutual consideration, care, synergy, willingness to make concessions, and unification of fiscal, monetary, and regulatory mechanisms.

Not only are ties of mutual guarantee necessary, but a country that will not follow that principle, and will not consider the needs of the rest of the countries, will actually be hurting itself. Stronger countries must assist the international system by using international rescue and aid funds.

The conceptual change of values will motivate restructuring of the international economy, where one country helps another, or the entire system, because all countries understand that if they do not, they will harm themselves due to the tight interrelations in the system.

At the same time there must be education and provision of information about the global, connected reality into which the international system has evolved. This will gradually change the worldview of the world population and its decision-makers. As a result, the new nature of the international economy will not be perceived as a necessary evil, but as a new idea that holds within it vast economic and social potential for the entire world.

Moreover, we must understand that the global economy is a reflection of international relations. For this reason, the change that is required first and foremost is a conceptual change of the relations among them. This would require constructing ties of mutual guarantee among countries based on the needs of each one, along with the needs of the entire international system.

This will manifest in expansive collaboration and solidarity among countries.

As said above, the economy reflects the social ties among individuals and nations. Therefore, changing the relations on the international level, and adapting the ties to the global and interdependent nature of the global economic system will yield the anticipated change from a threatening global crisis into a balanced and sustainable international economy. This will be radically different from the one we know today. The change of values is necessary for the improvement of both international and interpersonal relations.

To summarize, economics is a science that reflects the interrelations among people. The new economy, which is suited to the global and integral world, is radically different from the one we have today.

The economic crisis is a threat to all of us. All attempts to cope with it using traditional economic means have failed. The only hope of achieving economic balance is by implementing mutual guarantee. The global crisis results from the chasm between the competitive and individualistic nature of the current system, and the one that must exist in a global and integral system. That crisis will also accelerate the transformation.

Leading economists are already beginning to understand that the predisposition to hold on to the existing system even when it is failing is not serving our interests. Instead, we must focus on building a good, harmonious, and solid reality.

It is important to note that a pathway toward a balanced, harmonious, and steady economy does not imply revolution. Rather, it implies deliberation, transparency of information and decision-making processes, and clearer explanations and education about the laws of our new global-integral world.

MUTUAL GUARANTEE AS A PRACTICAL SOLUTION

IS MUTUAL GUARANTEE A PRACTICAL SOLUTION TO THE SOCIAL AND ECONOMIC PROBLEMS IN THE WORLD?

Key Points

- Monetary and fiscal attempts of unprecedented scope over the last few years have not driven the global economy out of its deep crisis.
- The current economic crisis is not only a natural extension of the crisis of 2008, but is bigger and more threatening than the former. This is due to our focusing on (and improperly treating) the symptoms, instead of diagnosing and treating the root of the crisis.
- Traditional economic solutions are based on principles incongruent with the new economy required to succeed in the global-integral world with its resulting interdependence.

- The only practical solution to the crisis is to shift our relationships into those of mutual guarantee (where all are guarantors of each other's well-being) as a basis for a balanced, functioning, and sustainable economy.
- Facilitating a supportive environment through educating and providing information are necessary so we can connect in mutual guarantee.

No Dispute over the Economic and Financial Crisis Being Global

The current economic and financial crisis is on the mind of every economist and decision-maker throughout the world. Almost against their will, they have come to terms with the fact that a global shift is happening, the outcome of a world-turned-global-and-connected, where each person and each country affects and is affected by all the others. In our new world, all of us are part of a single, global, continuously tightening network of economic, financial, and social ties—some overt, some covert.

The economic interdependence among countries prevents any one country, even those whose economy seems currently sound, like Germany, China, or Brazil, from avoiding the ramifications of the global crisis and the domino effect that brings this crisis to their doorsteps.

Thus, China is experiencing a slowdown in its growth because the chief buyers of its products—the U.S. and Europe—are under a severe crisis that affects private consumption and consumers' standards of living.

Germany, the strongest economy in Europe, could also face hardships due to the imminent collapse of the Greek economy and the subsequent chain reaction in the PIIGS countries (Portugal, Italy, Ireland, Greece, and Spain), and in the rest of Europe.

THE TRADITIONAL "TOOLBOX" HAS FAILED

Presidents, prime ministers, finance ministers, and chiefs of central banks throughout the world have been trying to heal the global financial markets and the economy since 2008. Not surprisingly, all the aid programs, healing plans, and economic incentives attempted worldwide relied on a single, old, and familiar economic paradigm that states that the solution to the crisis lies in a combination of monetary expansion (interest rate cuts) and fiscal expansions (increase of government expanses and pouring of funds into the market). The only differences between these solutions were in the amount of money poured in and the amount of expansion taken.

- **Monetary expansion** manifests primarily in interest rate cuts under the assumption that increasing the supply of cheap money will encourage commercial activity and private consumption, and thus boost growth and employment.
- **Fiscal expansion** means increasing government intervention in economic activities by increasing public expenditures, pouring funds into the market, tax cuts, and other government incentives. Increasing the government deficit to encourage economic activity is seen as a necessary evil and aims at those places where the "invisible hand" mechanism and the forces of the free market have failed.

TREATING NEW PROBLEMS WITH OLD SOLUTIONS

Two key problems exemplify the failed attempts to rescue economies from the global crisis:

1. All are based on the same paradigm, combining fiscal and monetary expansions. The theoretical basis for the

current economic paradigm was established in the early 1900s and has changed very little. However, since then the economic and the financial systems have radically changed. The process of globalization has accelerated exponentially, bringing with it growing financial risks wrought by the development of technology, abundance of cheap funding for speculations, financial engineering, and greed. Experts are struggling to accurately assess the risks embedded in such a global financial system. The human element is its most unpredictable component, along with mankind's uninhibited desire to maximize profits. Classical economic theories are unable to deal with the new challenges that the world is facing. The interrelations among financial markets, the real economy, and the firms' activities only complicate the picture and make it even harder to find a suitable solution inside the familiar arsenal.

2. The race to find "practical solutions" continues to fail. "Practical" means something that can be measured and quantified. People expect suggested changes in the budget, in the interest rates, in division of resources, in tax cuts, in imbalance between direct and indirect taxes, in school curricula, in welfare, mortgages subsidies and so forth. However, without a thorough understanding of the reasons for the crisis and the required changes in human interrelations in the current global and integral reality, these solutions will fail.

An aggregate of "practical" solutions of unprecedented scope in both budget and character, undertaken worldwide by both governments and central banks over the last three years, have failed to produce the anticipated result. The current global economic crisis is not only a natural extension of the crisis of 2008, but is bigger and more threatening. All U.S. government recovery plans[19] since 2008 have not only failed, but aggravated the crisis because they prevented us from treating its roots, and planted in us false hopes. Those plans settled for trying to cope only with the symptoms of the crisis rather than with its actual causes.

THE FAILED "PRACTICAL" STEPS IN THE UNITED STATES

To tackle the crisis of 2008, three rescue plans of unprecedented magnitude were launched, the first by the Bush administration, and the latter two by President Obama.

- On October 3, 2008, with the specter of the collapse of the Lehman Brothers investment bank just a few weeks prior, the U.S. government enacted the Troubled Asset Relief Program (TARP). The government purchased "toxic" assets and equity from financial institutions to bail the financial sector out of a likely default. In that program alone, the government was permitted to spend up to 700 billion dollars to save its financial sector. However, that colossal amount of money would soon be seen as grossly insufficient as the crisis continued to escalate.
- On February 13, 2009, in the wake of TARP's failure to secure the American economy, the Congress passed the American Recovery and Reinvestment Act of 2009 (ARRA)[20] at the urging of President Obama. The President believed that if he poured up to 787 billion dollars into the American economy, nationalized banks, lowered tax rates, and supported the financial industry he would

19   http://www.recovery.gov/Pages/default.aspx
20   http://www.recovery.gov/About/Pages/The_Act.aspx

resolve the crisis. He also tightened regulation of the financial industry to rein in the financial "wizardry" that had accelerated the popping of the bubble in 2008 and made it far more painful. ARRA failed, as well.

- In 2010, a second, bigger than the first, recovery plan was launched. It was called the American Recovery and Reinvestment Act, Federal Stimulus Funding in the January 2010 Financial Plan,[21] and relied on the same principles of increasing government deficit and pouring funds into the financial system, into firms and households. The American Recovery and Reinvestment Act was yet another failure.

But toward the end of 2011, President Obama launched a fourth, and different, kind of plan. The American Jobs Act[22] focused on the U.S. job market by offering 450 billion dollars' worth of tax incentives. The results of that plan remain to be seen.

Along with the government, the Federal Reserve Bank (FED) is working to support the economy. It lowered the interest rate to nearly 0%, believing (based on the traditional laws of economy) that by doing so and keeping it there long enough, the American economy would be revitalized because cheap money encourages spending and taking loans, and thus the economy would recover from the crisis. The interest rate has been near zero for almost three years now with no signs of relief from the crisis. In fact, it is only worsening. The FED proceeded to launch two giant-size incentive stimulus plans, which included buying an unprecedented 70% of American government bonds. This also failed.

---

21   http://www.nyc.gov/html/omb/downloads/pdf/jan10_fed_stim.pdf
22   http://www.whitehouse.gov/the-press-office/2011/09/08/fact-sheet-american-jobs-act

THE FAILED "PRACTICAL" STEPS IN EUROPE

In Europe, too, the European Central Bank (ECB) dropped the interest rate in the Eurozone from 4.25 to just 1 percent,[23] but that also proved futile.

The Eurozone established a European rescue fund with hundreds of billions of Euros to assist the more vulnerable countries in the bloc. This fund has struggled to raise money from its members. However, the demands for economic and social reforms that are conditions for receiving the funds are so harsh, they could cause widespread riots in the countries receiving them, as is happening in Greece.

At the end of 2011, in the wake of a real danger that Greece would default on its debt—which could lead to a dramatic escalation throughout the Eurozone and the world over—the principle of the fund was increased significantly to more than one trillion Euros. The agreement on the increase was signed after many challenging debates among the Eurozone countries. Many experts believe this attempt, too, will fail to resolve the sovereign debt crisis in Europe. At best, it will slightly delay the financial and possibly social collapse.

The International Monetary Fund (IMF) also jumped in to assist Europe, allocating substantial budgets for that purpose. Many countries in Europe also began to "tighten their belts" to reduce the deficit and meet the conditions for receiving aid from the funds. The cuts in those countries are hampering their abilities to put their economies back on track. In consequence, the cuts are actually worsening the situation in many countries. This situation has created a snowball effect, escalating rather than diminishing the problem. Now, the integrity of the entire Eurozone is in imminent danger.

---

23   "Euro Area Interest Rate," *Trading Economics*, http://www.tradingeconomics.com/euro-area/interest-rate

The Eurozone bloc, which was meant to provide mutual guarantee among its members, is about to collapse from the domino effect that began in Greece and is quickly spreading to Italy, Spain, Portugal. From there, it is only a matter of time before it affects the stronger economies of France and Germany.

Unemployment in much of the Eurozone is very high: In Spain, the unemployment rate of the total labor force is more than 20%, and among young academics, the unemployment soars to approximately 45%.[24] Many firms and sovereign states are approaching a state of default on their debts, and the protests against austerity plans testify to the complexity of Europe's plight.

In the U.S., unemployment is also high[25] and the national debt is skyrocketing.[26] Economic activity is slow and struggling toward recovery, while housing prices are still falling. In 2011, the U.S. suffered its first ever downgrade of its perfect debt rating,[27] and all the money markets in the world are paying heavily for it.

Although the American debt ceiling has been raised, to avoid increasing the deficit, any additional government aid or tax cuts must be accompanied by budget cuts. Another option would be to raise taxes in other sections of the economy. The unbounded credit that President Obama had to deal with the crisis has been lost, and henceforth, he will have to cut and tighten the belt. This undermines his ability to rescue the faltering American economy from the crisis.

Additionally, the American political system is battered and divided, poverty is rising, and private consumption—the primary

---

24   "Spain Unemployment rate," *Index Mundi*, http://www.indexmundi.com/spain/unemployment_rate.html
25   "United States Unemployment Rate," *Trading Economics*, http://www.tradingeconomics.com/united-states/unemployment-rate
26   "The Debt to the Penny and Who Holds It," http://www.treasurydirect.gov/NP/BPDLogin?application=np
27   "Instant view: U.S. loses AAA credit rating from S&P," *Reuters* (August 5, 2011), http://www.reuters.com/article/2011/08/06/us-usa-debt-downgrade-view-idUSTRE77504J20110806

growth engine of the American economy—is flatlining. It appears that America's economy has reached a dead end.

What Now?

After more than three years of failed attempts to heal the economies and financial markets throughout the world, it's clearly time for us to reexamine our tendency to apply familiar, yet evidently ineffective solutions to the current problems.

The conclusion we can make from the failure of every bailout and rescue plan, on the one hand, and the tenacity and severity of the economic and financial crisis, on the other hand, is that the existing paradigm has exhausted itself. Therefore, we must urgently adopt a new one. The current toolbox for resolving the crisis has failed and will continue to do so because it is inadequate to dealing with the economic-social global network on which we are all dependent.

If we adapt the economic and financial systems to that network of economic and social connections, if economics will also adapt, and if we acquire the characteristics of the new economy—the economy of mutual guarantee, then we'll find before us the tools to resolve the crisis.

The inability to deal with the global crisis has brought many people to agree that the real cause of the crisis is not the economy, but our human relations. In a *Der Spiegel* interview, Christine Lagarde, managing director of the IMF, said "There has been a clear crisis of confidence that has seriously aggravated the situation."[28]

Many agree that a change of concepts and values is required now, a shift from relationships based on power—aiming to maximize personal or national gain—to solidarity and social cohesion. The connection among people is *the* topic on the public agenda, and that is what requires mending and adjusting

28   "There Has Been a Clear Crisis of Confidence," *Spiegel Online International* (April 9, 2011), http://www.spiegel.de/international/world/0,1518,784115,00.html

to the laws of the global and connected world. The economy is meant only to support and maintain that connection among people; after all, it is we humans who create the economy, not the economy that creates a society.

The economy is not a law of Nature. It is a product of people's views and a reflection of human relations and interests. Therefore, to change the economy, we must first change ourselves and our relationships. We can induce change in the economy and society by agreeing that mutual guarantee is the foundation for the social-economic-educational system in each country, and in fact, in the entire world.

There is no argument that the socioeconomic situation is seriously flawed, and that the yearning for social justice has merit. One must ask, "What prevents those who see that the root of the problem lies in lack of mutual guarantee from understanding that therein lies the solution to all our problems?"

The answer is, "It's the inability to understand that such a shift of mindset is the most practical step we can take. This is attainable by creating a social and media environment that explains and educates about the value of mutual guarantee. Without this shift, no economic or social service plan will succeed."

Indeed, only one key element is missing in all the rescue plans: mutual guarantee—a genuine care for one another and agreement in a round-table type of decision-making process, feeling that we must all help one another and make concessions, just like a family. Without that necessary shift of mindset, as good as any new rescue package may seem, it will invariably fail.

THE BENEFITS OF AN ECONOMY BASED ON MUTUAL GUARANTEE

The new, mutual guarantee economy has several advantages. It is the only one that allows true and sustainable social justice to exist between the state and its citizens, and between states.

A mutual guarantee economy will be steady, characterized by substantial *voluntary* diminishing of social and economic gaps, and a decline in the cost of living.

It is easy to imagine the economic and social systems at the end of the transformation that the global crisis is imposing on us. Let's take a look at some of them.

In the mutual guarantee economy, society will adapt to the global network of connections. As a result, the financial bubbles and the endless race for speculative profits will change, leading to a healthy, balanced, and global economy that relies on global systems of trade, production, consumption, division of surplus and resources, international aid systems, and a healthier and less demanding way of life. Certainly this would be in stark contrast to the rat race we are in today.

Private consumption will return to sanity, instead of the excessive consumption that feeds on advertising and social pressure, with the sole aim to persuade us to consume redundant products and services. The mutual guarantee society will follow the principle of acting as guarantors of each other's well-being, and the economy will derive from it. It will manifest harmony among its members in fair trade partnerships, funds and resources focusing on progress, welfare, social justice, and a fair division of resources, rather than military defense and arms.

Instead of unrestrained competition among firms and countries, mutual support for the common good will prevail.

THE ECONOMY WILL CHANGE WHEN WE CREATE AN ENVIRONMENT THAT PROMOTES MUTUAL GUARANTEE

The key to shifting our relationships in a better direction lies in informing and educating children and adults alike. We must create a change-supportive environment that can help people adjust to the global-integral reality and achieve mutual guarantee among us. As a result, the principle of mutual guarantee will be the basis of all future systems, whether political, social, or economic.

Recent studies[29] have shown that our environments have a critical impact on our values, habits, and even our health. If we build an environment that is integral by nature, we will have a clearer picture of how to shift successfully from the current socioeconomic system, which has inflicted the current crisis upon us, to the new system, based on solidarity, mutual guarantee, and mutual harmony, extending to our dealings with the Earth.

29   The most notable studies are probably those published in the book, *Connected: The Surprising Power of Our Social Networks and How They Shape Our Lives—How Your Friends' Friends' Friends Affect Everything You Feel, Think, and Do*, by Dr. Nicholas A. Christakis and Prof. James Fowler (NY: Back Bay Books, 2011), see chapter, "Benefits of the New Economy."

CRISIS AS AN OPPORTUNITY

BEYOND HEALING THE ECONOMY, WE CAN USE THIS CRISIS TO LAUNCH A NEW ERA IN HUMAN SOCIETY

Key Points

- The global crisis has been the result of humankind's evolutionary path.
- The crisis affects many areas of our lives, such as education, family, and ecology, but we have not properly addressed it. The outbreak of the economic crisis forces us to take immediate action to ensure our survival.
- Globalization and the integration of the global system have rendered the old paradigms irrelevant. Therefore, we must develop new paradigms that suit the laws of the global-integral world.
- The crisis is an opportunity for worldwide introspection, as well as for improving our interpersonal and international relations.

- By closing the gap between the rules of the global-integral world—which compels us to connect among us in mutual guarantee—and the competitive, individualistic current economy, we will create economic well-being and a stable and harmonious society.

In medicine, diagnosing an illness is considered a good thing. It allows us to pinpoint the problem and treat it. The same applies to the economy. The economic and financial crises are global, affecting virtually every country in the world. It is hard to estimate the overall damage wrought by the crisis, as we are nowhere near its end. However, it is clear that the crisis is a continuation of the downturn of 2008, and has emerged as the greatest economic and financial challenge the world has faced since the 1930s' Great Depression. How governments, federal banks, and international financial institutions handle this evolving, expanding crisis will have a major impact on the future of the planet.

Every crisis presents an opportunity. The current one presents an opportunity to examine the state of the global economy, the global financial system, the state of financial relationships in the international system, as well as the social relations within each country, and even within individual businesses. Introspection is not a process performed while in a state of euphoria. Rather, it is done during periods of distress and crisis.

In truth, the global crisis is not confined to the economy. It is just as acute in education, domestic issues such as divorce and domestic violence, ecology, and the dwindling natural resources of the Earth. Every so often Nature "reminds" us of our fragility through an earthquake, a tsunami, a hurricane, or some other natural disaster. The immediate, forbidding effect of the global financial crisis makes the ideal wake-up call for us to reconsider the premises on which our economies, and our societies, are based.

THE CHALLENGES POSED BY GLOBALIZATION

The Great Depression of the 1930s and the failure to resolve it with the paradigms of classical economics led economist John Maynard Keynes (1883-1946) to develop the Keynesian model. This model asserts that to assure economic growth, there must be active government intervention in the financial markets.

Eight decades later, the Keynesian model has proven itself a failure. It has not resolved today's global economic crisis, which began as a financial crisis and evolved into a worldwide crisis of the real economy, reflected in unemployment, salary cuts, and social disorders. The failure of the old, familiar financial models led Nobel Prize Laureate, Joseph Stiglitz, to declare, "In a way, not only there is a crisis in our economy, there ought to be a crisis in economics."[30]

However, for a new economic paradigm to succeed, it must take into account the new conditions that have arisen in human society during the 21st century. The world has become a global village in which interdependence and mutual influence among its parts are growing. We have become a global-integral system, comprised of interconnected elements, obliged to be tied to one another, thus affecting one another and affecting the future generations—for the most part, adversely.

Thus, according to a report[31] by the Sustainable Europe Research Institute (SERI), "Humans today extract and use around 50% more natural resources than only 30 years ago, at about 60 billion tons of raw materials a year. ...Given current trends of growth, our extraction of natural resources could increase to 100 billion tons by 2030."

---

30   "Short films from the 2011 Lindau Nobel Laureate Meeting in Economic Sciences," *The New Palgrave Dictionary of Economics Online*, http://www.dictionaryofeconomics.com/ resources/news_lindau_meeting (the above-mentioned statement is in Stiglitz's video after 10:05 minutes.

31   "Overconsumption? Our use of the world's natural resources," *Sustainable Europe Research Institute (SERI)* (September 2009), www.foeeurope.org/publications/2009/ Overconsumption_Sep09.pdf

Another adverse effect of globalization is a concentration of power and wealth. According to a press release by Credit Suisse,[32] "Less than 1% of the world's adult population ... own 38.5% of global household wealth." This taps into the core arguments of the Occupy Movement that has emerged in the Fall of 2011 in numerous cities across the U.S. and around the world.

Much has been said about the repercussions of globalization. Thomas Friedman, author of *the World Is Flat: A brief history of the twenty-first century*, introduced in his October 11, 2011 *The New York Times* column[33] two theories that represent both ends of the debate over the impact of globalization. The first theory is that of Australian environmentalist, Paul Gilding, author of *The Great Disruption*. Gilding said, "I look at the world as an integrated system, so I don't see these protests, or the debt crisis, or inequality, or the economy, or the climate going weird, in isolation—I see our system in the painful process of breaking down," which is what he means by "The Great Disruption," said Gilding. "Our system of economic growth, of ineffective democracy, of overloading planet earth—our system—is eating itself alive."

An opposing theory is that of John Hagel III, who sees the current situation as the beginning of a "big shift," stemming from a combination of globalization and the Information Revolution. According to Hagel, today is the beginning of a time of thriving for humanity, albeit today we feel it as pressing, due to our continued use of inefficient institutions and practices.

At the end of the day, according to Hagel, we are in the midst of a vast global flow of ideas, innovations, and opportunities for profit through collaboration. Hagel believes that the great task ahead "...calls on us to learn faster by working together and to pull out of ourselves more of our true potential, both individually

---

32   "Credit Suisse: Global wealth has soared 14% since 2010 to USD 231 trillion with the strongest growth in emerging markets," *Credit Suisse* (October 19, 2011), https://www.credit-suisse.com/news/en/media_release.jsp?ns=41874

33   Thomas Friedman, "Something's Happening Here," *The New York Times* (October 11, 2011), http://www.nytimes.com/2011/10/12/opinion/theres-something-happening-here.html?_r=3&hp

and collectively." Whether we lean toward one theory or the other, both show us that the crisis has arrived just in time to be a wake-up call.

Indeed, we are called upon to adjust the economic and social systems to the requirements of today's global-integral system. However, to realize our potential, we need to make a fundamental shift in the thought processes and financial conduct that led us into the crisis. Just as the Great Depression of the 1930s led Keynes to form a more suitable economic paradigm for his era, we must change our current paradigms and adapt them to the reality of a global and integral world if we wish to emerge stronger from the current crisis. The crisis enables us to see that in today's world, the old paradigms have become dysfunctional, and the best example is the capitalistic paradigm.

CAPITALISM IN THE TIME OF GLOBALIZATION

The global crisis has put two of the tenets of capitalism to a test—one they seem to be failing. Those tenets are 1) that supply and demand balance themselves, and 2) that by working in one's own interest, an individual actually benefits the public. To pinpoint the issue let's return to the origins of capitalistic thought.

In his 1776 book, *The Wealth of Nations*, Adam Smith wrote, "As every individual ... endeavors as much as he can both to employ his capital in the support of domestic industry, and so to direct that industry that its produce may be of the greatest value; every individual necessarily labors to render the annual revenue of the society as great as he can.

"He generally, indeed, neither intends to promote the public interest, nor knows how much he is promoting it. By preferring the support of domestic to that of foreign industry, he intends only his own security; and by directing that industry in such a manner as its produce may be of the greatest value, he intends only his own gain, and he is in this, as in many other cases, led by an invisible hand to promote an end which was no part of his intention.

"Nor is it always the worse for the society that it was no part of it. **By pursuing his own interest he frequently promotes that of the society more effectually than when he really intends to promote it.**"[34]

For this reason, adds Smith, "The demand for those who live by wages, therefore, necessarily increases with the increase of the revenue and stock of every country, and cannot possibly increase without it. The increase of revenue and stock is the increase of national wealth."

Smith's assumption that supply and demand balance themselves through an "invisible hand" created the rule that leads capitalistic thinking to this day—that the individual's goal to maximize profits leads to maximum profit for the entire society. However, the primary development of contemporary economic thinking—as a necessary precondition for an efficient free market—is free competition. The market must include an unbounded number of manufacturers and consumers, all of whom posses all the relevant information, none of whom has any effect on the prices in the market, and the cost of transportation of goods is inconsequential in relation to the trade itself.

Those conditions were supposed to manifest in the most ideal manner in our global world. The development of global trade increased the number of manufacturers and consumers in the market, and significantly lowered the cost of transportation of goods. The Information Revolution via the internet contributed significantly to an increase in competitiveness. It also presented the required information to manufacturers and consumers.

Given these developments, one would expect that we would be experiencing the free market economy in its glory. How, then, did we end up in a global crisis that we can't seem to resolve?

---

34   The text in bold was emphasized by author of this essay

The reason for the emergence of the global crisis is this: while globalization increases the chances of certain classical assumptions to manifest, it also helps undermine another supposition, the one regarding the connection and mutual effect of the elements in the market. In a world where the free market is behaving according to Smith's ideal, people work in their own interest and are neither affected by others nor affect their well-being. Yet, people do not live in an isolated bubble. They are social beings whose well-being is interdependent with that of others, and that interdependence is experienced today more than ever before. This influence of social relationships introduces an element that is seemingly missing from Smith's theory.

Multiple studies describe the social integration that the world is currently undergoing, all part of the process of globalization. Among the most noted is the study of Dr. Nicholas A. Christakis and Professor James Fowler, made famous in their book, *Connected: The Surprising Power of Our Social Networks and How They Shape Our Lives—How Your Friends' Friends' Friends Affect Everything You Feel, Think, and Do*. They conclude that "The spread of influence in social networks obeys what we call the Three Degrees of Influence Rule. Everything we do or say tends to ripple through our network, having an impact on our friends (one degree), our friends' friends (two degrees), and even our friends' friends' friends (three degrees). ...Likewise, we are influenced by friends within three degrees."[35]

Thus, our health, wealth, and happiness are largely a function of what people three degrees of remoteness from us think and do.

In a similar vein, Professor Ludger Kühnhardt, director of the Center for European Integration Studies in Bonn, stated, "The 21st century, unlike the period after the Congress of

35   Nicholas A. Christakis and James Fowler, *Connected: The Surprising Power of Our Social Networks and How They Shape Our Lives—How Your Friends' Friends' Friends Affect Everything You Feel, Think, and Do* (NY: Back Bay Books, 2011), 26

Vienna, is no longer a zero-sum game of winners and losers. Rather, it is a century of multiple networked nodes."[36]

NEGATIVE EXTERNALITIES

One example of the influence of human interconnectedness on economic dynamics is called "negative externalities." This term describes the cost inflicted upon others by an action to which those affected have no connection. Thus, if a factory pollutes a nearby lake, killing the fish in that lake, it inflicts harm on the fishermen whose livelihoods depend on the fish in the lake. This is a negative externality.

The traditional solution involves supervision by authorities. Yet, overproduction and over- pollution abound despite the supervision and the mounting evidence that we are living in an interconnected and interdependent world. The methods that leaders and decision-makers are trying to apply to deal with the problems of our interconnected world are the same methods they have used for decades, when the world was far less interconnected.

The question, then, is not whether decision-makers will have to revamp their approaches to solving the global crisis, but how much taxpayers will have to pay before they realize it and act on it.

INTO THE FUTURE

The failure of capitalism, as expressed in the current crisis, demonstrates our urgent need to build a new economic paradigm. The heads of the Organization for Economic Co-operation and Development (OECD) and the International Labor Organization (ILO) recently issued a warning that "The

---

36   Ludger Kühnhardt, "A Call for the United States to Rediscover Its Ideals," *The Globalist* (May 24, 2011), http://www.theglobalist.com/StoryId.aspx?StoryId=9149

overall number of unemployed is still at 200 million worldwide, close to the peak recorded at the depth of the Great Recession."[37]

Even in the G20 countries, "The analysis ... expresses concern that employment may ... grow at a rate of just under one per cent (0.8) until the end of 2012, resulting in a 40 million job shortfall in G20 countries next year [2012] and a much larger shortfall by 2015."

In light of the perilous future, rising food prices, and the intensification of social unrest throughout the world, it is clear that a new paradigm is required, one that suits the new, globally interconnected world of the 21st century. The new paradigm must take into account the integral and interdependent nature of the world today. Instead of the obsolete concept that man's selfishness will ultimately lead to greater common good, we need to see humanity as a complex entity with interdependent elements.

Moreover, the rate at which the crisis is spreading indicates that the window of opportunity is closing. We are living on borrowed time and must hasten our steps toward the transformation. The only question is, "What kind of transformation should that be?"

One possible answer can be found in the words of Pascal Lamy, Director-General of the World Trade Organization (WTO).[38] "The real challenge today is to change our way of thinking—not just our systems, institutions or policies. We need the imagination to grasp the immense promise—and challenge—of the interconnected world we have created. The future lies with more globalization, not less — more co-operation, more interaction between peoples and cultures, an even greater sharing of responsibilities and interests." In his closing words,

---

37   "ILO warns of major G20 labour market decline in 2012 and serious jobs shortfall by 2015," *International Labor Organization* (September 26, 2011), http://www.ilo.org/global/about-the-ilo/press-and-media-centre/news/WCMS_163835/lang--en/index.htm

38   Pascal Lamy, "Lamy underlines need for 'unity in our global diversity,'" *WTO NEWS* (June 14, 2011), http://www.wto.org/english/news_e/sppl_e/sppl194_e.htm

Lamy predicted, "The future lies with more globalization, not less—more cooperation, more interaction between peoples and cultures, and even greater sharing of responsibilities and interests. It is 'unity in our global diversity'... that we need today."

PUTTING WORDS INTO ACTION

The new world is pushing people closer, forcing us to care for one another in genuine solidarity, and to rethink aggressive competition and excessive consumerism. This crisis is leading us, kicking and screaming, into harmony with the laws of the global-integral system.

To adapt to this global-integral world, we must study how it works, how all the elements are connected in industry, in banking, and in government systems. Therefore, the key to success lies in a new system of education that will inform people of the nature of the world today. This program will not only inform, but also help us practice new codes of communication and human relations, thus showing us how to build our social relations to survive in an interconnected world.

As noted by Lamy, the continued evolution of humanity toward globalization and integration is a certainty. If we learn how to adjust our interrelations and economy to the new reality, we can achieve harmony and balance with the laws of the new system. This new balance will consist of mutual guarantee (each person guaranteeing others' well-being), social solidarity, genuinely free education for all, a reframing of how we use our natural resources, and harmony in the global economy.

As long as we retain our current perception of the world, we will lack understanding of the essence of the change the world is undergoing. Only if we reeducate ourselves and learn about the new reality will we understand its causes and the nature of the change required of us. Through education, we will grasp that we must overcome the elements that separate us on all levels, and that we must seek ties of mutual guarantee. When we achieve that, we will discover that the new reality is also a giant opportunity. The transformation of thought is the key to our success and to global prosperity. And without this global crisis, we would never deem such a transformation desirable or even feasible.

RESEARCH IN ECONOMICS CHALLENGES THE EQUATION THAT WEALTH EQUALS HAPPINESS

THE KEY TO HAPPINESS IS NOT WEALTH, BUT A CONNECTION OF MUTUAL GUARANTEE AMONG US

Key Points

- Studies prove that beyond a certain income, additional income does not necessarily increase happiness.
- When we achieve a goal we set for ourselves, the satisfaction is brief and fleeting.
- Measuring personal well-being and quality of life by the growth of gross product distorts the real picture.
- Other measurements, such as the value of human relations, can represent personal happiness more successfully.
- Educating toward mutual guarantee and social solidarity will change human relations.

THE STUDY OF HAPPINESS

The maxim, "Money can't buy happiness," was confirmed in a number of studies in economy and psychology. These studies show that despite the increase in the standard of living and wealth in industrialized countries, the level of happiness remains stagnant. In 1974, Professor of Economics at University of Southern California, Richard A. Easterlin, published a groundbreaking study.

The publication, "Does Economic Growth Improve the Human Lot? Some Empirical Evidence,"[39] established what is now known as "The Easterlin Paradox," a key concept in happiness economics. The paradox asserts that in international comparisons, the average reported level of happiness does not vary much with national income per person, at least for countries with income sufficient to meet basic needs. Easterlin argued that personal happiness does not depend on people's absolute income, but on their *relative* one. People are unhappy not because they are poor, but because they are (or perceive themselves to be) at the bottom of a scale by which they measure themselves.

Below is a diagram demonstrating average income compared to happiness in the United States, 1957-2002, released by The World Watch Institute in 2004[40]:

---

39   Richard A. Easterlin, "Does Economic Growth Improve the Human Lot? Some Empirical Evidence," *University of Pennsylvania* (1974), http://graphics8.nytimes.com/images/2008/04/16/business/Easterlin1974.pdf
40   Brian Halweil and Lisa Mastny (project directors), *State of the World 2004: A Worldwatch Institute Report on Progress Toward a Sustainable Society*, Linda Starke, Editor (N.Y., W.W. Norton & Company, Inc., 2004), http://ec-web.elthamcollege.vic.edu.au/snrlibrary/resources/subjects/geography/world_watch_institute/pdf/ESW040.pdf, Figure 8-1, p 166

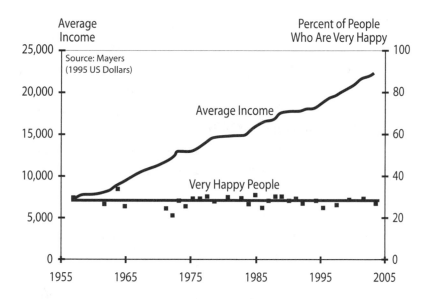

Easterlin was not the only one who doubted that a successful economy is measured by the growth of the Gross National Product (GNP) and the parameters related to it. In a lecture on *TED, Ideas Worth Spreading*,[41] Nic Marks, founder of the Centre for Well-Being at the New Economics Foundation (NEF), made some very poignant arguments regarding how we measure happiness. "How crazy is that that our measure of progress, our dominant measure of progress in society, is measuring everything except that which makes life worthwhile [well-being]? One of the problems we face ... is that the only people that have cornered the market in terms of progress is a financial definition of what progress is, an economic definition ... that somehow, if we get the right numbers to go up, we're going to be better off, ...that somehow life is going to get better. This is somehow appealing to human greed ... that more is better. Come on. In the Western world, we have enough."

41   Nic Marks, "The Happy Planet Index," *TED, Ideas Worth Spreading* (July 2010), http://www.ted.com/talks/nic_marks_the_happy_planet_index.html

THE ECONOMIC CRISIS AS AN OPPORTUNITY TO EXAMINE THE ECONOMIC PARADIGM

The study of happiness is becoming more pertinent than ever in these days of global crisis. The equation: wealth = happiness is at the basis of the existing economic paradigms. To a great extent, it determines our way of life, its quality, our interpersonal relationships, and relations between citizens and state. To a great extent, the belief that wealth=happiness also affects the nature of the entire international economic system.

Every college freshman understands that the expression, "Maximizing utility under an existing budget limit," is tantamount to the maximum level of happiness that can be obtained with a given sum of money. The contemporary crisis is an opportunity to examine whether the current economic paradigm and existing life-systems truly achieve their goals and provide people with happiness.

REALITY VS. THE AMERICAN DREAM

In his 1931 book, *The Epic of America*, American writer and historian James Truslow Adams, coined the term, "The American Dream." He wrote, "Life should be better and richer and fuller for every man, with opportunity for each according to his ability or achievement."[42]

That dream has become the aspiration not only of every child and adult in America, but the dream of billions throughout the world. This dream translates into the belief that to be happy, one must have a home of one's own, preferably a large, single-family home in a good neighborhood, two cars per family, and substantial savings for the golden years. In that dream, every new arrival to America can become wealthy and prosperous if only he or she works hard enough.

---

42   James Truslow Adams, *The Epic of America*
(U.S.A. Taylor & Francis, 1935), 415

Unfortunately, today's reality is not The American Dream. In reality, tens of millions in America cannot work hard and make their dreams come true simply because they cannot get a job. The healthcare and welfare systems are so unequal and warped that they only perpetuate the socioeconomic inequalities. In truth, only few people realize The American Dream while the rest continue to struggle to avert poverty.

But the biggest surprise about The American Dream is not that only a few make that dream come true. Rather, it is the fact that even those who *do* succeed are not any happier!

HAPPINESS—NOT AN EXACT SCIENCE

Tal Ben Shahar is a PhD in organizational behavior and a renowned teacher and writer on positive psychology and leadership. He claims that the root of negative sensations is internal—an erroneous concept of happiness that causes prolonged frustration. In an interview with the Israeli newspaper, *Calcalist*, he says, "Successful people often experience higher levels of depression or dissatisfaction. The main reason for it is that the mechanism operating within many of us makes us think that when we obtain something—a raise, a new car, or a new house—we will be happy. That way, we live with the sensation that we have something to look for. The problem is that when we obtain the goal we had set, the sensation of satisfaction and joy we derive is temporary and quickly fades. We experience an increase in the level of happiness, but we quickly return to the place from which came before we obtained what we wanted, except now we are disappointed, and sometimes lost. That mechanism of happiness is faulty from the core. Paradoxically, it makes us far more unhappy, particularly when we obtain what we want."[43]

---

43   Tal Ben Shahar, "Our Happiness Scheme is Wrong, and Then Comes Frustration, *Calcalist* (April 17, 2011), http://www.calcalist.co.il/local/articles/0,7340,L-3515186,00.html

THE NEIGHBOR'S GRASS IS GREENER

Another reason for the gap between income and happiness is our tendency to measure ourselves compared to others, more commonly known as "Keeping up with the Joneses." Numerous studies in behavioral economics show that people behave irrationally when they compare themselves to others. As economists David Hemenway and Sara Solnick demonstrated in a study at Harvard University, many people would prefer to receive an annual salary of $50,000 when others are making $25,000, than earn $100,000 a year when others are making $200,000.[44] Similarly, economists Daniel Zizzo and Andrew Oswald conducted a study that showed that people would give up money if doing so would cause someone else to give up a slightly larger sum.[45]

WEALTH MEANS FINANCIAL SECURITY—OR DOES IT?

Studies were conducted to determine whether a person with a higher income would have fewer worries, compared to a person who could hardly make ends meet. The results were fascinating. Professor of behavioral economics at Princeton University, Talya Miron-Shatz, tested the connection between the level of income and one's sense of financial security. She found that "Financial security adds to the prediction of life satisfaction above the contribution of income."[46]

---

44   Solnick, S.J., & Hemenway, D., (1998). "Is more always better? A survey on positional concerns." *Journal of Economic Behavior & Organization*, 37 (3), 373-383.
45   The study is quoted in an online essay, "Misery Loves Company: Recession Edition," in the blog, *Macro and Other Market Musings* (December 27, 2008), http://macromarketmusings.blogspot.com/2008/12/misery-loves-company-recession-edition.html
46   Talya Miron-Shatz, "'Am I going to be happy and financially stable?': How American women feel when they think about financial security," *Judgment and Decision Making*, vol. 4, no. 1, February 2009, Princeton University, pp. 102-112 (http://journal.sjdm.org/9118/jdm9118.html#note1)

The World Is Changing, and So Is the Perception of Happiness

The findings in the above-mentioned studies, and in many more, challenge the most fundamental conventions in our society. We are beginning to realize that the current equation of money = happiness is simply not true. Instead, the pursuit of wealth causes frustration, harms our health, and damages our relations with others by cultivating competition and self-centeredness. Our thinking is beginning to change from an individualistic and competitive one to one that is more balanced and harmonious with the environment and with others.

Our behavior as consumers, our attitude toward money, and the satisfactions ascribed to having money are all beginning to adjust themselves to the global and interconnected reality we live in, where we are all tied to one another, affecting one another like pieces in a global puzzle. In that system, which can be called "global-integral," we are beginning to feel the emptiness of the values of consumerism and the pursuit of material goods. Those who do strive for them and believe that money means happiness are beginning to realize that the traditional methods to obtain that happiness are no longer working because the world has changed into a global-integral unit. For this reason, we cannot arrive at happiness if it is not tied to the happiness of others, and certainly not if it comes at others' expense.

Capitalism and Happiness—Not What You Thought

On January 20, 2011, Prof. of Political Economy, Robert Skidelsky, a member of the British House of Lords, and author of a prize-winning biography of the economist John Maynard Keynes, wrote,[47] "Capitalism may be close to exhausting its potential to create a better life, at least in the world's rich countries. By 'better,' I mean better ethically, not materially. ...It was, and is, a

---

47   Robert Skidelsky, "Life after Capitalism," *Project Syndicate* (January 20, 2011), http://www.project-syndicate.org/commentary/skidelsky37/English

superb system for overcoming scarcity. By organizing production efficiently, and directing it to the pursuit of welfare rather than power, it has lifted a large part of the world out of poverty.

"Yet what happens to such a system when scarcity has been turned to plenty? Does it just go on producing more of the same, stimulating jaded appetites with new gadgets, thrills, and excitements? How much longer can this continue? Do we spend the next century wallowing in triviality?...

"Indeed, the 'spirit of capitalism' entered human affairs rather late in history. Before then... A person who devoted his life to making money was not regarded as a good role model. ...It was only in the 18th century that greed became morally respectable. ...This inspired the American way of life, where money always talks.

"The end of capitalism means simply the end of the urge to listen to it. People would start to enjoy what they have, instead of always wanting more. ...As more and more people find themselves with enough, one might expect the spirit of gain to lose its social approbation. Capitalism would have done its work, and the profit motive would resume its place in the rogues' gallery.

"...The evidence suggests that economies would be more stable and citizens happier if wealth and income were more evenly distributed. The economic justification for large income inequalities—the need to stimulate people to be more productive—collapses when growth ceases to be so important.

"Perhaps socialism was not an alternative to capitalism, but its heir. It will inherit the earth not by dispossessing the rich of their property, but by providing motives and incentives for behavior that are unconnected with the further accumulation of wealth."

THE ECONOMY AS A REFLECTION OF HUMAN RELATIONS

The reason why the assumption that a large income means more happiness does not reflect reality is because we have forgotten that economics includes a dominant human element. It is a complex element, not an exact science. And most of all, it is hard to measure the human element.

Behavioral economics has already proven that man is not a rational machine. In 1979, Professors Daniel Kahneman and Amos Tversky presented the "Prospect" theory, for which Kahneman won the Nobel Prize in economics (six years after Tversky's death). Their research showed that people are incapable of analyzing complex decision situations when the future consequence is uncertain. Instead, they rely on short cuts that seem to make sense, or rules-of-thumb, with few people evaluating their underlying probability.[48]

The above-mentioned studies of Hemenway and Solnick, as well as many other studies, indicate that economics concerns human relations just as much as it explores how humans conduct their business.

THE SOLUTION—RELATIONS BASED ON MUTUAL GUARANTEE

By most indicators, mankind has reached a tipping point. Despair and depression have become far too prevalent worldwide. In Europe, a study revealed that, "Nearly 40 percent of Europeans are mentally ill."[49]

Drug and alcohol abuse are on the rise and the divorce rate throughout the Western world is skyrocketing. The data clearly show that we are becoming hopeless, insecure, and pessimistic, even about the prospect of our children having a better life than

48   Daniel Kahneman, *Encyclopædia Britannica*, http://www.britannica.com/EBchecked/topic/891306/Daniel-Kahneman
49   "Fast 40 Prozent der Europäer sind psychisch krank" (translation: "Nearly 40 percent of Europeans are mentally ill"), *Der Spiegel* (September 5, 2011), http://www.spiegel.de/wissenschaft/medizin/0,1518,784400,00.html

our own.[50] This trend has existed for some years now, even in more economically optimistic times, but the current crisis is accelerating and intensifying the trend toward pessimism.

So what can make us happy? Clearly, every person needs to have sufficient income for dignified sustenance, allowing for the necessities of life to be met, such as food, clothing, housing, healthcare, and education. But beyond that, as was demonstrated above, a rise in well-being is possible only by improving human relations, not by increasing personal wealth. We need to shift from an attitude of alienation to one of consideration and of mutual guarantee, where all are guarantors of each other's well-being.

With a world turned global and closely integrated, we must adjust our connections accordingly. We must come to feel that social and economic systems and human interactions are based on care, consideration, and mutual guarantee. When people feel confident that they will not be exploited or used, they lower their walls of defense against others. In other words, we need mutual guarantee in order to be happy, and mutual guarantee cannot be bought with money.

The significance of the studies presented above and of others similar to them is that they prove that wealth is not a precondition for happiness. Rather, consideration, care, mutual guarantee, and financial security are better means for obtaining happiness than merely being rich. If we can create an environment that instills values of solidarity, care for others, and mutual responsibility, we will be able to increase the personal level of happiness of every person in society. This is why mutual guarantee is so important.

We are not born equal—some are born smarter, some stronger, some wealthier, and some with more robust health.

---

50   Toby Helm, "Most Britons believe children will have worse lives than their parents – poll," *The Guardian* (December 3, 2011), http://www.guardian.co.uk/society/2011/dec/03/britons-children-lives-parents-poll?INTCMP=SRCH

As long as society continues to tell us that we must compete with others, exceed them in money and resources, we will not achieve social equality, and in a global-integral world, social equality and mutual guarantee are preconditions for *personal* happiness. To resolve the mental, emotional, economic, and financial problems of our world, we must create a society based on a network of mutual guarantee, in which each person partakes in the activities of society and receives from it what he or she needs for reasonable sustenance. When we create such a society, it will allow for genuine equality, and the sense of injustice and depravity that prevail in today's social climate will be all but gone.

The key to the solution lies in cultivating values of generosity, consideration, and mutual care to replace the values of materialism and competitiveness. This will enhance feelings of happiness, as well. We will discover that realizing our full potential is possible only in a society that conducts itself by the principle of mutual guarantee. The satisfaction, confidence, and security we will derive from living in a harmonious society will bring us the happiness we crave and have been unable to achieve through monetary means.

TOWARD BALANCED CONSUMERISM IN THE NEW ECONOMY

OVER-CONSUMPTION AND ITS ILLS WILL GIVE WAY TO BALANCED, FUNCTIONAL CONSUMPTION AND A HEALTHIER WAY OF LIFE

Key Points

- Over the last 50 years, consumer consumption has become a key element in our lives. Today it determines our social status.
- The advertising industry, which works to maximize the profits of giant consortiums, as well as its own, has created a culture of consumption known as "consumerism," and made us into modern slaves.
- The rat race of consumerism adversely affects many aspects of our lives—our physical and mental health, our family ties, our free time, and our environment.
- The solution is to shift to balanced, functional consumption, after which many brands and products will disappear.

- The transition into balanced consumption is part of a structural change into a balanced and functional economy where both the economy and balanced consumption are founded on values of mutual guarantee and social solidarity.
- A functional economy and balanced consumption will provide for our reasonable needs. With their time and resources freed up, people will be able to realize their personal and social potential and be able to maintain a harmonious and sustainable way of life.
- Providing information and education, and creating supportive environments are necessary for us to connect in mutual guarantee.

FROM CONSUMPTION TO CONSUMERISM

The term "consumption" is defined as "the using up of goods and services" to satisfy man's needs. In Neoclassical Economics, an individual gains the more he or she personally consumes. The economic theory deals with the behavior of the homo-economicus (economic human) and one's relations with one's environment.

The Rational Choice Theory[51] presents individuals as rational beings acting to realize their interests, having all the tools and reasoning required to make objective decisions in order to maximize their personal gain. In fact, however, these assumptions are not realized. The latest studies in behavioral economics demonstrate that man does *not* behave rationally.

Prof. Dan Ariely, an international expert in behavioral economics, describes in his book, *Predictably Irrational: The Hidden Forces That Shape Our Decisions*, many incidents of such irrational behavior. One example deals with a person who was willing to make a 15-minute drive to save seven dollars on a pen

---

51   John Scott, "Rational Choice Theory," from *Understanding Contemporary Society: Theories of The Present*, edited by G. Browning, A. Halcli, and F. Webster. (U.K., Sage Publications, 2000), http://www.soc.iastate.edu/sapp/soc401rationalchoice.pdf

that cost $25, but would not drive 15 minutes to save the same seven dollars for a $455 suit.[52]

Our aspirations have grown along with technological and industrial advancements. Over time, the world has adopted the "culture of consumption," otherwise known as "consumerism." This implies acquisition of goods and services *not* for satisfying fundamental needs, but for obtaining social status. Thus, the product has become a symbol of one's social status, and the product itself and its usability are of very little importance. Buying the product may well bring more pleasure to the buyer than its actual use.

In the modern consumer society, happiness has become a function of one's level of consumption, while consumption itself has become the objective of our lives. Barbara Kruger, an American conceptual artist, memorialized the consumer society with her piece in the Museum of Modern Art—a paper shopping bag with the words: "I shop, therefore I am"—paraphrasing Descartes' famous words describing the essence of man: "I think, therefore I am." Man has become a compulsive consumer with a new pastime: shopping. Exaggerated consumption has become a culture, and one of contemporary society's primary characteristics.

WHO PROFITS FROM OVER-CONSUMPTION?

Consumerism is vigorously promoted by giant corporations, advertising agencies and the media, the goal being to sell us as many products as possible for the sole purpose of maximizing their profits.

The banking and financial systems willingly fund consumers, manufacturers, and advertisers, giving ostensibly cheap credit, which perpetuates the system. Consumerism also creates

---

52   Dan Ariely, *Predictably Irrational: The Hidden Forces That Shape Our Decisions* (NY, HarperCollins Publishers, 2008), 20.

substantial income for national budgets, as countries tax every link in the chain of consumption. That is, even the government has become an element that encourages excessive consumption and aspires to increase it. It engages in this for economic reasons and because the sense of abundance and numerous choices increase citizens' satisfaction with how the government functions thus enhancing its chances of being reelected.

According to Tim Jackson, Professor of Sustainable Development at the University of Surrey, England, "It's a story about us, people, being persuaded to spend money we don't have on things we don't need, to create impressions that won't last on people we don't care about."[53]

A prime example of this is the U.S., which "sanctifies" private consumption and whose system is built to preserve and enhance that consumption. Private consumption makes up approximately 70% of the GDP. It has become the primary growth engine of the American economy.

While the term, "consumerism," may sound "clean," perhaps even desirable for some less developed countries, it is simply a polite term for an addiction to shopping, superficial values, financial household recklessness, and questionable morals when it comes to prioritizing. We deplete our natural resources such as water and energy in order to produce needless things. We work longer hours chasing after money that eventually buys us redundancies that only provide transient satisfaction.

We call our work life "the rat race" or "modern day slavery." We have grown accustomed to communicating in brand names, using them to convey messages about our social and financial status. Which brands one buys, and how much of them, have become parameters that define one's standard of living. We use

---

53   Tim Jackson, "Tim Jackson's economic reality check," *TED, Ideas Worth Spreading* (October 2010), http://www.ted.com/talks/tim_jackson_s_economic_reality_check.html

it to learn about others—what they can afford, what they like, the social environment that they are in, and so on.

BUYING MORE, SAVING LESS

According to the magazine, *Global Finance*, "Household saving rates as percentage of disposable income in the U.S. has declined from 7.3 in 1992 to a mere 1.7 in 2007, at the start of the financial crisis."[54] People are squandering their savings and even increasing their debt to "stay in the game," with the full endorsement of the advertising industry.

Such a negative savings rate has grave social and financial repercussions. It is a time bomb that will explode in times of crisis when our financial confidence is compromised. When a rainy day comes, we often find ourselves with little or no savings, yet we must still pay for the credit we received to fund needless consumption. When such a turn takes place, people stop their over- consumption abruptly, causing companies to cut their work forces. Then, state income from taxes drops and the crisis quickly escalates.

THE 2008 CRISIS WAS DUE TO
AMERICANS' RECKLESS CONSUMPTION

A classic example of such an exploding time bomb is the housing bubble that inflated continually after the beginning of the 21st century. Until 2008, banks were tempting people to make loans even when they could not afford to repay them. They allowed applicants to buy houses with 100% funding, thus creating huge demands in the real-estate markets.

But banks did more than that. They enticed home buyers into refinancing their mortgages and taking still more loans, with their houses as collateral. At the time, the rising market

---

54   Tina Aridas, "Household Saving Rates," *Global Finance*, http://www.gfmag.com/tools/global-database/economic-data/10396-household-saving-rates.html#axzz1bQlyYiFq

value of the houses helped the banks increase consumption even more. Huge amounts of irresponsible credit flowed into the pockets of American citizens, who squandered more and more on goods and services, enjoying an irrational sensation of wealth and happiness.

Satisfaction with this lavish way of life became an economic modus operandi that was envied and emulated throughout the Western world. Accordingly, the American economy boasted impressive performances in those years due to excessive private consumption. The sensation of affluence was real and tangible, yet false, the brainchild of an economic model that had detached from reality and from realistic prices of real-estate and personal financial assets.

When the process finally exhausted itself, due to a combination of risky "financial engineering" on the part of banks and institutional investors, and speculation in the financial markets, everything ground to a halt, dragging the United States and the entire world economy into the worst financial crisis since the 1930s. In fact, we are still in the midst of the crisis now at the beginning of 2012.

EDUCATION FOR CONSUMERISM TURNS US INTO COMPULSIVE SHOPPERS

Consumerism has become a culture as a result of the kind of education that most people receive. Education begins with the parents' personal example, as well as that of friends and the environment as a whole. Each of us lives in a certain environment and absorbs its values and conduct. A major part of our education is through exposure to commercials in the media—both overt and covert—as well as other manipulations that advertisers and manufacturers impose on us. The strong influence of advertising urges us to align with the values of consumerism that permeate society. These values become part of our internal landscape, falsely defining our levels of happiness, success, and social status.

Advertising began in the 19th century and was dramatically transformed in the 20th century. In the 19th century, advertising appealed to our sense of reason, emphasizing the advantages of the products for potential buyers. But in the 20th century, advertising shifted from rational to emotional and sensual. Commercials began to sell "better living" instead of promoting the goods themselves. The commercials we see today are actually saying, "You may feel bad now, but if you buy our product, you will feel better."

Author and filmmaker, Dr. Jean Kilbourne, said in the film, *The Ad and the Ego*, "Ads sell a great deal more than products. They sell values, images, and concepts of success and worth, love and sexuality, popularity and normalcy. They tell us who we are and who we should be." Each day, we are exposed to hundreds of commercials that encourage us to consume more and more. A study published in the magazine, *Media Matters*, reveals that "Today's typical adult gets about 600-625 chances to be exposed to ads in one form or another per day."[55]

Commercials encourage us to increase our buying as proof of our success, as well as a way we can obtain happiness and satisfaction. In fact, consumption has shifted from providing us with reasonably comfortable living, to consumption for the sake of obtaining social status.

CONSUMPTION MEANS HAPPINESS~OR DOES IT?

Imagine how much a new car would delight you. We enjoy examining the options—the model, the color, the advantages and disadvantages, speaking to people about it and reading about it on the internet. Finally, the day arrives and we are certain that

---

55   "Our Rising Ad Dosage: It's Not as Oppressive as Some Think," *Media Matters* (February 15, 2007): 1-2, https://www.mediadynamicsinc.com/UserFiles/File/MM_Archives/Media%20Matters%2021507.pdf

in a few hours we will be the owners of the car we've dreamed of for months—or even years. We are certain that this car will make us happy for at least for the next ten years. Yet, research proves otherwise. In a study titled, "Affective Forecasting," Professors Timothy D. Wilson and Daniel T. Gilbert of Harvard University write that we have a "…tendency to overestimate the duration of one's future emotional reactions,"[56] and that we "[do] not make very accurate forecasts about their reactions to future events."

In other words, a new car is not likely to make us happy for the next ten years. Instead, it is quite likely that within six months, possibly less, it will turn from a dream-come-true into another piece of our dreary daily lives. And this will drive us into the next purchase. It is a frustrating vicious cycle, which our social environment encourages.

Renowned expert on Positive Psychology, Dr. Tal Ben-Shahar, points out, "The problem is that when we achieve the goal we set out for ourselves, the sensation of joy and fulfillment derived from it is transient. We experience a spike in our level of happiness, but soon return to our place prior to obtaining what we wanted, except now we are disappointed, sometimes even lost."[57]

Further, according to Dr. Ben-Shahar, "We are mistaken to think that if we get a raise or a new car we'll be happier. That gives us a sense that we have something to look for. However, while ambition and hard work may upgrade us financially, they will not grant us lasting happiness. The sensations of satisfaction and joy are transient."

The Easterlin Paradox, presented in the previous chapter, is a key concept in the field of happiness economics. Easterlin's

---

56   Timothy D. Wilson and Daniel T. Gilbert, "Affective Forecasting," *Advances in Experimental Social Psychology*, vol. 35 (USA, Elsevier Science, 2003): 349, 395, url: http://www.abdn.ac.uk/~psy423/dept/HomePage/Level_3_Social_Psych_files/Wilson%26Gilbert(2003).pdf
57   Tal Ben Shahar, "Our Happiness Scheme is Wrong, and Then Comes Frustration, *Calcalist* (April 17, 2011), http://www.calcalist.co.il/local/articles/0,7340,L-3515186,00.html

theory proposes that beyond a certain level, economic growth and an increase in the average income do not induce an average increase in the happiness of the population. The effect of income on our happiness is felt when we compare our income to that of others.

OVER-CONSUMPTION AND THE ECOLOGICAL CRISIS

According to a 2011 survey by the UN Department of Economic and Social Affairs, titled, "The Great Green Technological Transformation,"[58] progress has enabled us to raise the standard of living of the world population. However, at the same time it has damaged the environment. To date, half the forests on Earth have been cut down, a substantial portion of the drinking water has either been pumped out or polluted, and numerous species of plants and animals are becoming extinct. Additionally, global warming is likely to cause a fivefold increase in the number of natural disasters compared to the year 1970.

A report by The Sustainable Europe Research Institute (SERI)[59] indicates that uninhibited consumption of natural resources such as water, fertile land, forests, oil, gas, and coal is inflicting ecological damage in catastrophic proportions, creating a drastic change in the Earth's climate. According to the report, "Humans today extract and use around 50% more natural resources than only 30 years ago, at about 60 billion tons of raw materials a year."

A report by The Climate Institute in Australia[60] states, "Climate change will have many adverse impacts on Australians'

---

58   *World Economic and Social Survey 2011: The Great Green Technological Transformation, The United Nations Department of Economic and Social Affairs* (Printed at the United Nations, New York, 2011), http://www.un.org/en/development/desa/policy/wess/wess_current/2011wess.pdf

59   "Overconsumption? Our use of the world's natural resources," *Sustainable Europe Research Institute (SERI)* (September 2009), www.foeeurope.org/publications/2009/Overconsumption_Sep09.pdf

60   "A Climate of Suffering: the real costs of living with inaction on climate change," *The Climate Institute* (Melbourne & Sydney, The Climate Institute, 2011), http://www.climateinstitute.org.au/images/reports/tci_aclimateofsuffering_august2011_web.pdf

health—physical risks, infectious diseases, heat related ill effects, food safety and nutritional risks, mental health problems and premature deaths. The emerging burden of climate-related impacts on community morale and mental health—bereavement, depression, post event stress disorders, and the tragedy of self-harm—is large, especially in vulnerable rural areas. Across all sectors of the Australian population, mental health ... is vulnerable to the stresses and disruptions caused by a changing climate and its environmental and social impacts."

FROM CONSUMERISM TO BALANCED CONSUMPTION

The solution is clear. Each of us must support a decrease in the present excessive consumption that has long become a key aspect of our lives, and that of the global economy. Instead, we must encourage balanced consumption. As this transition unfolds, private consumption will return to more sustainable levels, replacing the unrestrained gobbling fueled by commercials and social pressures. Many redundant products will disappear and consumption will return to a focus on practical usage. Instead of brands as symbols of social status, the degree of one's contribution to the community and general well-being will determine one's position in society. By reducing demand, prices will drop, and dignified living will finally become affordable for all.

Balanced consumption is an important part of the new economy—the balanced one. Adjusting the connections among people to the interdependence in the global-integral world will alter the entire economic system, not only consumption. It will shift from a competitive economy that is bloated and self-centered into a balanced, stable, functional, and sustainable form, bearing altruistic characteristics. Every system will be finely tuned to provide for the entire human race on a reasonable level, no more but also no less.

We have already stated that consumerism has many flaws. The recurring financial and social crises indicate that very soon we will be forced to shift from our current pattern. We can no longer afford to increase consumption indefinitely because we are paying heavily for it, attempting to finance our demanding lifestyles. The consumerism we have adopted is causing ongoing frustration without the ability to achieve the anticipated satisfaction.

The shift toward balanced consumption will "calm" our financial and social systems and balance our way of life. In fact, we can use the same tools that today preach excessive consumption to promote a more balanced approach. Using the existing media and advertising systems, we can alter society and build together an environment whose impact on us will change our priorities and the current, detrimental social values that we hold.

THE NEED FOR BROAD AGREEMENT ABOUT THE NATURE OF THE CHANGE

The necessary transition from our current excessive consumption to a balanced one cannot be dictated by the authorities. If it were, we would only aspire to return to the present system as soon as possible. Only if the transition to balanced consumption is accompanied by a conceptual change throughout society, via extensive education efforts and support from the social environment will we comprehend that the change is to our benefit. After a short adaptation period, we will feel it, too.

In the global, connected world where everyone depends on everyone else, there cannot be a continuing discrepancy between our current egoistic, competitive, and manipulative connections and the laws of the new system. In the new world, there is no place for inconsideration, lack of concern, and absence of mutual guarantee. The new, obligatory connections between us will help us change the entire economic and commercial systems. For example, producers will stop creating needless products, and will not talk us into buying unhealthy food just because it is profitable. In an economy that reflects the value of mutual guarantee among people, private consumption will regain its sanity.

This does not mean that we will return to the pre-industrial revolution era, or that this process is to be imposed on citizens by the government. Rather, this will be a natural process that life itself necessitates, a process of regaining normalcy from an out-of-control consumerism into consumption that matches the connections among us in a global and interconnected world.

THE ADVANTAGES OF BALANCED CONSUMPTION

Along with the transition to balanced consumption under the umbrella of the mutual guarantee, the numerous problems resulting from excessive consumption elaborated earlier will be solved. Additionally, we will discover the advantages of mutual guarantee:

1) Improved Health

Most of the food products we currently see on commercials do not contribute to our health. According to the World Health Organization (WHO),[61] in 1980, 1.5 billion adults suffered from overweight. By 2010, that number had doubled. Also, nearly 43 million children worldwide suffer from obesity, now ranked fifth in the list of fatal illnesses.

A group of British psychologists examined 281 children ages 6-13,[62] showing them a commercial for a toy and a commercial

---

61   "Obesity and overweight, Fact Sheet no. 311, *World Health Organization*, updated March 2011, http://www.who.int/mediacentre/factsheets/fs311/en/
62   Emma J. Boyland, PhD, Joanne A. Harrold, PhD, Tim C. Kirkham, PhD, Catherine

for a certain food product. Then they asked the children to name their favorite foods. The majority of the children chose foods that contained more fats and carbohydrates after watching the commercial for food than after watching the commercial for a toy.

The American Academy of Pediatrics published a Policy Statement[63] in regard to watching TV and obesity among children and youths. The pediatricians call for a ban on commercials for fast food on child-oriented TV programs.

2) Improving the Ecological Situation and the State of Natural Resources

Reducing the consumption and production of redundant products will contribute to a significant improvement in our environment by reducing air and water pollution and reducing the amount of waste and exploitation of natural resources and energy.

We tend to treat gas, oil, coal, and other resources as if they will always be here. But will we be able to use these resources without any accountability in the future? According to data from www.worldometers.info, at the current rate of consumption we will be completely out of oil by approximately 2050, assuming we don't increase our consumption of it even more than today!

By shifting to balanced consumption, we will be able to maintain a decent lifestyle, our industrial activity will return to its natural size, and we will stop producing needless products. When that happens, we will have achieved balance and harmony, first among ourselves and then between the Earth and us. Mutual guarantee as an economic treaty, therefore, carries significant

Corker, BSc, Jenna Cuddy, Sca, Deborah Evans, BSc, Terence M. Dovey, PhD, Clare L. Lawton, PhD, John E. Blundell, PhD, and Jason C. G. Halford, PhD, "Food Commercials Increase Preference for Energy-Dense Foods, Particularly in Children Who Watch More Television," *Pediatrics* (March 9, 2011), http://pediatrics.aappublications.org/content/128/1/e93
63   "Policy Statement—Children, Adolescents, Obesity, and the Media, *Pediatrics* 2011;128;201; originally published online June 27, 2011; DOI: 10.1542/peds.2011-1066, now available at http://pediatrics.aappublications.org/content/128/1/201.full.html

benefits to the human race, both as a solution to the world crisis and as a springboard to head off the escalating ecological crisis.

3) Lowering the Cost of Living

Advertising takes up a substantial part of the cost of a product. Returning to balanced consumption will reduce the demand for many products and brands. Consequently, some of them will disappear and others will become more affordable. The advertising industry will shrink to its natural size, and if we use advertising and environmental influences wisely, we will be able to reduce the cost of products significantly.

Also, in an environment of mutual guarantee, producers and importers will accept a more reasonable profit margin and will no longer seek to profit at the expense of consumers. Accordingly, the prices of products and services will decline to just above their production cost.

Incidentally, there is no need to worry about the advertising industry. It will serve as a key means to convey educational messages and to build a supportive environment for the value of mutual guarantee.

4) More Leisure

Once we stop pursuing unrestrained consumption, we will be able to shorten our workday and make time for what really matters: our family and social connections, learning various life skills, and generally enjoying our lives. The environment that we will design through the media will explain to us how to live, raise children, and function in the new world in a way that realizes the personal and social potential within each of us.

5) Improved Family Ties

When we have more free time, we will be able to dedicate more time to being with family and friends, rather than working 10-

12 hours a day. Additionally, the change of values in society will prevent frequent arguments with children who demand we buy them more new brands that they see in commercials or in the hands of their friends.

A CHANGE THROUGH EDUCATION, INFORMATION, AND THE INFLUENCE OF THE ENVIRONMENT

For one who is born into a consumer-oriented environment, a change to a balanced society, the cessation of producing redundant products, and a relinquishing of shopping as the favorite pastime may be seen as a bleak forecast, as economic and cultural regressions. Economists might argue that the global GDP will drop and with it governments' ability to care for the needs of their citizens.

However, with the help of a broad educational framework, including the dissemination of information and the creation of a change-supportive environment, we will learn the new rules of the game in the global and integral world. Finally, we will understand that abandoning over-consumption in favor of a balanced version is not only an imperative process, but an irreversible one. Closing the gap between the way we live and the dependence among all of us in the new world will have many positive social and economic effects. The current method has collapsed, and the global crisis is indisputable evidence of that. And finally, a new, balanced world is rising.

BENEFITS OF THE NEW ECONOMY

A BALANCED ECONOMY IS NOT ONLY MANDATORY IN THE GLOBAL AND INTEGRAL REALITY, IT ALSO BENEFITS US ALL

Key Points

- An economy based on the principles of mutual guarantee is congruent with the laws of the global-integral system, and will therefore be stable and best provide for our reasonable needs of sustenance. It will also allow us to make time to realize our personal and social potentials.

- An economy under the umbrella of mutual guarantee has many social and economic advantages, such as a fair standard of living for all, reduction of the cost of living, transparency, a larger "economic pie," and a dramatic reduction of gaps and economic inequality.

- The transition from today's competitive, self-centered economy to a balanced, functional one will reveal many surpluses in money, assets, and resources that can be used for the public benefit.

• The transition to a mutual guarantee-based economy will be gradual, but from its inception a positive dynamic of change and hope will be created—a new spirit, a sense of cohesion and personal confidence.

AN ESCALATING CRISIS IN EUROPE AND THE UNITED STATES

The global economic crisis is rapidly worsening. The United States suffered its first ever downgrade of its credit rating, and the Eurozone is threatening to collapse altogether, or alternately, face insolvency of sovereign debt, which would shake up financial markets all over the world. At the same time, leading economists are making foreboding statements, such as Nouriel Roubini's, "There's a significant probability ... that over the next 12 months, there's going to be another recession in most advanced economies,"[64] or Joseph E. Stiglitz's, "In a way, not only there is a crisis in our economy, there ought to be a crisis in economics."[65]

The economic interdependence among countries makes it impossible for them to isolate themselves and resolve their problems separately. An example of that is the attempt of the Eurozone to save the faltering Greek economy. The Polish Finance Minister, Jacek Rostowski, speaking before the European Parliament, warned that "Europe is in danger, and the breakdown of the Eurozone would lead to a chain reaction leading to the breakup of the European Union (EU) and ultimately to the return of war in Europe."[66] Also, German Chancellor Angela Merkel stated that

---

64   Nouriel Roubini, "ROUBINI: Ignore The Recent Economic Data — There's Still More Than A 50% Chance Of Recession," *Bussiness Insider* (October 25, 2011), http://articles.businessinsider.com/2011-10-25/markets/30318837_1_double-dip-recession-eurozone-ecri
65   "Short films from the 2011 Lindau Nobel Laureate Meeting in Economic Sciences," *The New Palgrave Dictionary of Economics Online*, http://www.dictionaryofeconomics.com/resources/news_lindau_meeting (the above-mentioned statement is in Stiglitz's video after 10:05 minutes.
66   Amiel Ungar, "Polish Finance Minister Warns of War if EU Collapses," *Arutz Sheva* (September 16, 2011), http://www.israelnationalnews.com/News/News.aspx/147945#.TrUbyPSArqE

"Euro-region leaders must erect a firewall around Greece to avert a cascade of market attacks on other European states."[67]

Naturally, investors are concerned about the future of the world economy. During weekend talks of policy makers, investors and bankers in Washington, PIMCO, the world's largest bond investor, predicted, "Economies will stall over the next year as Europe slides into a recession."[68]

Regarding that same event, former U.S. Treasury Secretary, Lawrence Summers, said he has been to 20 years of International Monetary Fund (IMF) gatherings, and "There's not been a prior meeting at which matters have had more gravity, and at which I've been more concerned about the future of the global economy."

Unemployment in Europe and the United States is high and rising. For example, Spain's unemployment rate rose sharply to a new Eurozone high of 21.3 percent in the first quarter of the year, with a record 4.9 million people out of work.[69] In the United States, the unemployment rate is 8.6, with 13.3 million people out of work.[70]

THE ECONOMY NEEDS A MAKEOVER

The failure to resolve the global crisis that began in 2008 baffles the most prominent economists and exposes the limitations of the current economic paradigms. The expansive monetary policy was meant to reverse the decline and gradually heal the world economy, but the reverse seems to have happened. It appears that the economic "toolbox" in the hands of decision-

67   Sebastian Boyd, "Chilean Peso Advances After Merkel Urges Firewall Around Greece," *Bloomberg* (September 26, 2011), http://www.businessweek.com/news/2011-09-26/chilean-peso-advances-after-merkel-urges-firewall-around-greece.html
68   Simon Kennedy, Rich Miller and Gabi Thesing, "Pimco sees Europe sliding into recession," *Financial Post* (September 26, 2011), http://business.financialpost.com/2011/09/26/pimco-sees-europe-sliding-into-recession/
69   Daniel Woolls, "Spain's Unemployment Rate Hits New Eurozone Record Of 21.3 Percent," *Huffington Post* (April 29, 2011), http://www.huffingtonpost.com/2011/04/29/span-unemployment-inflation-economy-debt_n_855341.html
70   United States Department of Labor, Bureau of Labor Statistics, www.bls.gov/news.release/empsit.nr0.htm

makers treated only the symptoms of the crisis rather than the crisis itself.

The interest rate cuts, expansion of budgets—intended to boost industry and commerce—tax cuts, reforms in finance, interference of central banks in bond and currency markets have all failed to reinvigorate the stalled economy.

To resolve the crisis, we must first diagnose the root of the problem and adopt a solution that corrects it. Treating only the symptoms doesn't resolve the crisis itself, as its recent re-emergence indicates.

At its very heart, the economy is an expression of how we relate to each other. In the current economy, our primary motive is to maximize our profits in a competitive environment that perpetuates in us the sense of lack. This results in a zero-sum-game, where one's gain comes at the expense of another.

The solution to the economic crisis requires us to first change our relationships into those based on mutual guarantee. Such a change will be possible only by creating a supportive environment, including information systems that educate us about this change. These will include use of the media, as well as adult and youth education systems. The educational framework will endorse such values as solidarity, collaboration, empathy, care for others, and mutual guarantee.

Social sciences provide ample proof of how the environment influences people.[71] Hence, we must build a society that teaches us to think differently and to adopt prosocial values.

71   Perhaps the most notable examples are the studies published in the book, *Connected: The Surprising Power of Our Social Networks and How They Shape Our Lives—How Your Friends' Friends' Friends Affect Everything You Feel, Think, and Do*, by Dr. Nicholas A. Christakis and Prof. James Fowler:
Christakis, N. A.; Fowler, JH (22 May 2008). "The Collective Dynamics of Smoking in a Large Social Network" (PDF). *New England Journal of Medicine* 358 (21): 2249–2258.
Christakis, N. A.; Fowler, JH (26 July 2007). "The Spread of Obesity in a Large Social Network Over 32 Years" (PDF). *New England Journal of Medicine* 357 (4): 370–379
Fowler, J. H.; Christakis, N. A (3 January 2009). "Dynamic Spread of Happiness in a Large Social Network: Longitudinal Analysis Over 20 Years in the Framingham Heart Study"

Today, society rewards us with money, power, and glory. Such rewards create competition and induce aggressiveness as each of us tries to exploit or manipulate others on personal, company, national, or international levels. If the rewards were to change and, instead, encouraged mutual guarantee, the change would be easy to make and would have broad public support. This is the power of the environment to influence our behavior.

FIRST THINGS FIRST: PUTTING OUT THE FIRE

First, we must put out the fires and deal with the most pressing issues facing us. To do so, we must come together, deliberate in a round-table format, and discuss—just like a family—how we can help those among us who are in desperate need, living below the poverty line. Without a solution for such problems that we can all agree on, we cannot make any progress.

Agreement is a precondition of forming the mutual guarantee among us. Agreeing on mutual guarantee will enable the more fortunate to make the necessary concessions to assist others and create the economic amendments that will thoroughly deal with the challenges of poverty.

Some of the financing to mend the imbalance will come from state budgets, reflecting the change in socioeconomic priorities. However, the bulk of the money will come from new sources created by the transition from excessive consumerism to reasonable consumption. That transition will reflect the change from an individualistic, competitive economy to a collaborative, harmonious one that is in sync with the laws of the global, integral world.

At the same time, we must acquire basic life skills and initiate consumer education to qualify us to pursue an independent,

(PDF). *British Medical Journal* 337 (768): a2338.doi:10.1136/bmj.a2338. PMC 2600606. PMID 19056788.
Christakis, N. A.; Fowler, JH (26 July 2007). "The Spread of Obesity in a Large Social Network Over 32 Years" (PDF). *New England Journal of Medicine* 357 (4): 370–379

balanced way of living in the new world. Combining immediate economic and financial solutions with proper consumer education will act as "CPR" for the lower-income individuals in society. It will also forge the common basis necessary to adopt mutual guarantee as a social and economic treaty, tying us all together, in sync with the laws of the global-integral world.

Toward a New Economy, Under the Umbrella of Mutual Guarantee

It is easy to describe the improved socioeconomic system at the end of the transformation process, towards which this crisis is drawing us. The inadequacy of the current economic systems in the global network and the increasing personal and political interdependence are the real reasons for the escalating global crisis. When decision-makers and leading economists grasp that these are the core issues, the solution will become obvious, though we will still need to change our relations to those of mutual guarantee. Once accomplished, we can move to a new economy that reflects this shift of ideas and values in the world.

Under the umbrella of mutual guarantee, both the economy and human society will be in harmony with the global network of connections. Instead of "sailing against the wind," wasting energy and resources trying to maintain a failing economic method, a new economy will form, both balanced and stable, relying on solid social cohesion on all levels, expansive international cooperation, balanced consumption, and stable financial markets. This will be a far cry from the current financial markets, which produce destructive bubbles every 5-7 years.

Benefits of the Economy of Mutual Guarantee

There are many benefits to an economy based on mutual guarantee. By attempting to cling to the existing, failing economic model and ease the immediate problems following the financial crisis, we are making it harder to appreciate the vast potential of the mutual guarantee economy. If we imagine that we are already in a state of mutual guarantee, we will be able to see its many advantages:

1) **A just and fair standard of living for all:** An economic policy based on mutual consideration will help us allocate the necessary public funds to raise the lower classes above the poverty line. At the same time, workshops, life skills training and consumer science will help people develop financial independence. Living beyond our means and over-consumption have become a global liability that requires correction..[72,73]

2) **Lowering the cost of living:** When greed is no longer the basis of our economic relations, when each of us is content with a reasonable profit and does not aspire to maximize profit at the expense of others, the prices of products and services will drop to near-production cost. Today, the prices of many goods and services are too high because each link along the commercial chain strives to achieve maximum benefit. Extolling the value of mutual guarantee in communication networks and in the public discourse will make firms add public benefit to their equations. This will make life more affordable for all of us.

The first signs of a cost-lowering movement are already emerging. Social unrest is actually causing manufacturers to lower the prices of products and services. For now, these are variable, occasional, minor, and passing discounts,

---

72   "Average credit card debt per household with credit card debt: $15,799." By: Ben Woolsey and Matt Schulz, "Credit card statistics, industry facts, debt statistics," *CreditCards. com*, http://www.creditcards.com/credit-card-news/credit-card-industry-facts-personal-debt-statistics-1276.php#Credit-card-debt
73   "The average British adult already owes £29,500, about 123 per cent of average earnings." By: Jeff Randall, "The debt trap time bomb," *The Telegraph* (October 31, 2011), http://www.telegraph.co.uk/finance/comment/jeffrandall/8859082/The-debt-trap-time-bomb.html

but the trend is clear. When we transition to a relatively balanced consumption pattern, both demand and prices will be come down.

Also, diminishing the cost of living will diminish inequality and social gaps, one of the primary advantages of the mutual guarantee economy.

3) **Diminishing social gaps:** One of the primary ills of the present global economy is a constant increase in inequality. This is the prime initiator of the worldwide unrest that demands social justice. When we treat each other like family, we will not tolerate inequality of opportunity or means among us or anywhere in the world. Instead of unrest and fear of revolution and violence, the mutual guarantee economy will yield broad consent as economic gaps are diminished, and the stability of the system is enhanced.

Diminishing inequality means, among other things, economic and social concessions on the part of the top income earners. Education, the influence of the environment, and an effective mechanism of communication—such as the round table—will make certain that all decisions are reached with transparency and fairness, and reflect the social and economic consensus—imperative for mutual guarantee. In return for their concessions for the common good, those who make them will be rewarded with public appreciation for their contributions. Additionally, those who receive assistance and resources will be able to enjoy a better, more dignified life. They, too, will appreciate the new method.

4) **A genuine, thorough budget reform:** The only thing that can create a sense of social justice and mutual guarantee for each individual in society is the belief that we are all in the same boat, and must work together. This will require a fairer method of prioritizing in the national budget, reached by

broad consensus, not through the squabbles of lobbyists and pressure groups.

An economy managed with transparency will allow everyone to understand how decisions are made, and will even help people influence them. When we feel a sense of partnership and involvement, we no longer feel negative emotions such as the frustration that currently exists toward policy makers. This lessening of negativity will allow people to agree with and support the decisions made by decision-makers, even when some of their choices are not popular. The satisfaction of acting as one family that makes decisions at the round table will encourage us to make concessions to each other.

5) **Increasing the financial "pie":** If every citizen, business, and government office feels part of the global family, many extras will appear in money, goods and services, state and municipal budgets, and even in our personal budgets. Consider how many things we have at home that we never use. We can take our surplus food and clothing, give it to the poor, and put the financial extras toward covering a significant portion of others' current needs. This will not even require an increase in the budget deficit, or impose austerity means or taxes.

However, we are not suggesting charity as a solution, although charity is a great expression of a solid community life and mutual assistance. Rather, we are talking about efficacy. For example, according to a CNN report, 30% of all food produced in the world each year is wasted or lost. That's about 1.3 billion tons, according to a report by the U.N. Food and Agriculture Organization.[74]

Why can't countries where hunger is a real problem receive that surplus? The answer, in a word, is "interests."

---

74   Ramy Inocencio, "World wastes 30% of all food," *CNN Business 360* (May 13, 2011), http://business.blogs.cnn.com/2011/05/13/30-of-all-worlds-food-goes-to-waste/

Distributing the surplus food means increasing the supply, which would lead to lower prices. This, in turn, would diminish the profits of food producers and marketers. In an economy based on mutual guarantee, such a situation would be impossible. How can we throw away food when members of our family are starving?

This is just one example. For more examples of the benefits of mutual guarantee economy, see chapter, "Surplus and Improving Public Well-Being."

6) **Improving employer-employee relations and firm-government relations:** Research in behavioral psychology indicates that wealthy people seek respect, not money.[75] Yet, today companies and CEOs are evaluated based on their profits and gains. Greater profit means a higher ranking in rating firms or appearance on the list of "most successful CEOs of the year."

Possibly the best example of this narrow, self-centered thinking of maximizing profits is the U.S. job market. The reason why the American job market is not adding more jobs, even as the economy grows, is that firms prefer to increase their workers' overtime, or shift part-time workers into working full time, rather than hire new people.

Today, such considerations are considered logical. But in an economy conducted by mutual guarantee, the values will be such that more people will be able to share in the prosperity of the economy, rather than fewer people sharing more of the profits. Similar improvements will be made in companies' relations with the government and tax authorities, leading to fairer taxes and fewer tax evasions.

7) **Stability and long-term solutions:** The new economy will be based on the values of mutual guarantee, and will necessarily be consistent with today's global interdependence, Such an

75   Tay, L., & Diener, E., "Needs and subjective well-being around the world," *Journal of Personality and Social Psychology* (2011), 101(2), 354-365. doi:10.1037/a0023779

economic method, in harmony and balance with the global
and integral network, will be more stable and sustainable
than all the existing economic and social methods. It would
match its environment and reflect a broad consensus among
its elements: people, companies, and states. A balanced
economy that is friendly toward both man and Nature
would allow each person to live in dignity, to feel that the
system was personally "friendly," and to receive sufficient
sustenance, along with the opportunity to reciprocate by
contributing to the system.

8) **Certainty:** The transition to the new economy will be
gradual. At first, there will be dynamics of change and hope,
a new spirit in society, a sense of cohesion and personal
security. The current fear of being exploited will make way for
concessions and gestures of generosity in several areas, such
as more affordable housing prices, employment contracts
that do not exploit workers, a simpler bureaucracy that truly
serves the public interest, fair banks, and service providers
that actually provide the intended service at a sane price.
In short, people will feel confident in their interrelations,
a feeling so badly needed in these uncertain times, and one
that money truly cannot buy.

9) **True happiness:** The new economy will create in us a sense
of fulfillment that cannot be measured with money. As
described in the chapter, "Studies Challenge the Notion
that Money Means Happiness," beyond a certain level of
income, additional money does not improve one's feeling.
Instead, people get satisfaction from successful relationships,
from a sense of confidence and self-fulfillment. The new
economy and its benefits are not transient, but are solid
and stable because they are in sync with the laws of mutual
guarantee. These enable a decision-making process based
on a broad consensus.

10) **An applicable decision-making process:** As the new economy will be conducted with transparency, everyone will see how decisions are made and will be able to influence them. This is the only way to establish a practical decision-making process that will make people feel that decisions are both fair and unbiased, reached after thorough consideration of *everyone's* needs. This will also enhance the stability of the socio-economic system.

11) **Economic and financial stability:** Money markets have changed from a meeting ground for companies and investors into a battleground of aggressive global players, with enough power to rattle and shake global market in pursuit of "an extra buck," regardless of the soundness of the system. A mutual guarantee economy will allow money markets to regain their original function without repeatedly falling into financial bubbles that pop and lead to disaster in the real economy.

12) **Balanced consumption:** The pursuit of excessive consumption has long become a key element in our lives and in the world economy. In the mutual guarantee economy, this will gradually make way for balanced consumption. In fact, the process has already begun, thanks to the present crisis and the gradual transition from a competitive, wasteful, and unequal economy to a balanced, functional one whose goal is to provide for everyone's basic needs. Commercials and other forms of social pressure to convince us to buy redundant products and services will disappear, as will numerous superfluous brands and products. Instead, the desire to contribute to society and participate in community life for the common good will replace them as one's pride and joy.

Also, because of the decreased demand, prices will drop and reasonable, dignified living will become affordable to all. Companies will produce only what is truly necessary for us to lead a comfortable and balanced life as described in the chapter, "Toward Balanced Consumerism in the New Economy."

13) **Global balance and harmony:** The transition from excessive consumption to balanced buying will reveal that Earth contains sufficient resources to sustain all of us comfortably for many years to come. The exploitation of natural resources will stop, and we will discover Earth's magnificent rejuvenation abilities.

The stability of the mutual guarantee economy is based on strong social cohesion and mutual concern. That stability requires that we understand that in an era of globalization, our interdependence requires us to adapt our connections and our social and economic systems into a single, harmonious system. It will provide for the needs of all of humanity, and support and encourage everyone's needs to realize the great potential within them.

EMERGENCY PLAN FOR UNEMPLOYMENT

PROPER TREATMENT OF UNEMPLOYMENT CAN BECOME A SPRINGBOARD FOR PERSONAL AND NATIONAL ADVANCEMENT

Key Points

- In the modern society, work has become the center of our lives. Work-related parameters determine our social status.
- The economic crisis causes high unemployment in Europe and in the U.S., but is expected to rise even more. The statistics we are given aren't accurate; unemployment is higher than reported.
- The necessary transition from a competitive and overactive economy into a balanced, functional one will be followed by a dramatic contraction in the sectors of services, retail selling, and industry. Hundreds of millions of workers are expected to be ejected from the job market. Inflation rates will rise to the high double-digits.

- In a balanced economy, 20% of the population can provide for the sustenance of all of humanity.
- A rising unemployment rate is a social and economical time-bomb that threatens the stability of governments and the entire international system.
- As part of an emergency national mechanism, an education system must be created into which the unemployed will be admitted. Studying in that system will count as a job for which the government will grant a "sustenance scholarship" matched to the personal needs of each student as long as they continue to study in this system.
- The subjects to be taught at this system will include personal finance, necessary life skills in the new reality, the laws of the global-integral world and its effect on our lives, on society and on the economy, and the advantages of mutual guarantee as a way of life.
- The program will defuse the time-bomb and will allow governments to carry out the necessary transition to mutual guarantee and a balanced, sustainable economy.

IS LIFE ALL ABOUT WORK?

In the last 200 years, work has become more than a way to provide sustenance, raise children, and save for old age. Our jobs, positions, and incomes have become key elements in the self-esteem of many of us, as well as how we are perceived by society. Often, work is also a social framework, an indication of our personal success, and the seminal value by which we are brought up from an early age. One of the most common questions a child is asked is, "What do you want to be when you grow up?" Invariably, the answer involves an occupation. But why do children limit their answers to their dream jobs? Is working at this or that job, or having this or that profession, the height of our aspirations?

It seems like it is, today. And yet it wasn't always so. Until recently, work was just a way to make a living and provide for one's needs. However, The Industrial Revolution has made work the center point of our lives, and the process has continued to accelerate as capitalism expanded and evolved. Along with the significance of work in our lives, work-related stress has become a prevalent phenomenon. It seems to be a cycle in which we earn more, but we are also more emotionally tied to our jobs, which we perceive as key to our self-esteem.

If we lose our job, we try to do everything we can to get quickly back into the job market. Why? It seems to be more than just about money. Apparently, the real issue is that unemployment is tantamount to being a failure.

The significance of our work to enhance our self-esteem, and to obtain the appreciation society and family can offer us, are making unemployment a destructive phenomenon. When one becomes unemployed, one loses not only one's job, but one's self-esteem and social status.

THE IMPACT OF THE ECONOMIC CRISIS ON THE JOB MARKET

One of the most significant problems resulting from the global crisis is the rise in unemployment, due to low demands, a decline in private consumption, closing of factories, and staff cuts by employers. All of these have an immediate effect on the job market. Not only is the number of unemployed rising, but so is the decline in the number of jobs available.. Put differently, once a worker is laid off, it is harder to find a new job, which prolongs the unemployment period. Some of the unemployed are completely eliminated from the job market and stop looking for a job altogether because they have given up hope of find a job.

On September 26, 2011, the heads of the Organization for Economic Cooperation and Development (OECD) and the International Labor Organization (ILO) published a joint statement in which they expressed their concern over the seriousness of the jobs crisis, where "200 million people are out of work worldwide."[76] They also warned that "The job shortfall [in Europe] may increase [from 20 million] to even 40 million by the end of 2012."

In the U.S., the unemployment rate has only recently declined below the 9% threshold but is still very high.[77] In Europe, and especially among the PIIGS countries (Portugal, Italy, Ireland, Greece and Spain), unemployment is at its peak and in the double digits, with the exception of Italy.

Unemployment is at its worst among the young. According to an ILO report titled, *World of Work Report 2011: Making Markets Work for Jobs*, "Among countries with recently available data, more than one in five youth, i.e. 20 per cent, were unemployed as of the first quarter of 2011."[78] According to unemployment statistics from Eurostat, youth unemployment is rising dangerously high with rates of 21.4% in the euro area, the highest being in Spain (48.9%) and in Greece (45.1%).[79]

This report also emphasizes that the state of the job market poses an imminent risk to the political and social stability of many countries around the world. "As the recovery derails, social

76   "G20 Labour Ministerial: Joint Statement by OECD Secretary-General Angel Gurría and ILO Director-General Juan Somavia," *OECD*, (September 26, 2011), http://www.oecd.org/document/17/0,3746,en_21571361_44315115_48753169_1_1_1_1,00.html
77   "United States Unemployment Rate," *Trading Economics*, http://www.tradingeconomics.com/united-states/unemployment-rate
78   *World of Work Report 2011: making markets work for jobs* (International Institute for Labour Studies, 2011), ISBN, 978-92-9014-975-0, http://www.ilo.org/wcmsp5/groups/public/---dgreports/---dcomm/---publ/documents/publication/wcms_166021.pdf, p 7
79   "Unemployment statistics," *European Commission, Eurostat*, http://epp.eurostat.ec.europa.eu/statistics_explained/index.php/Unemployment_statistics

discontent is now becoming more widespread. ...In 40 per cent of the 119 countries for which estimates could be performed, the risk of social unrest has increased significantly since 2010. Similarly, 58 per cent of countries show an increase in the percentage of people who report a worsening of standards of living. And confidence in the ability of national governments to address the situation has weakened in half the countries.

"The Report shows that the trends in social discontent are associated with both the employment developments and perceptions that the burden of the crisis is shared unevenly. Social discontent has increased in advanced economies, Middle-East and North Africa."[80]

Indeed, we have already seen the impact of economic crises on societies and governments in countries such as Egypt, Yemen, Libya, or—to a lesser extent—Spain and Italy, and even in the U.S. with the Occupy Movement, and Israel, with the protests in the summer of 2011.

In addition to the growing tension in many countries, the traditional fiscal and monetary solutions to the crises in general, and to the unemployment in particular, seem ineffective as the national debt of many countries has bloated to perilous proportions. This threatens the solvency of many countries, as well as hinders governments' abilities to cope with social problems such as unemployment. In such a state, unemployment is expected to rise much higher, distress to worsen, and social unrest to break out at intensities that may well pose an imminent threat to the stability of governments and the entire international system.

80   *World of Work Report 2011: making markets work for jobs* (International Institute for Labour Studies, 2011), ISBN, 978-92-9014-975-0, http://www.ilo.org/wcmsp5/groups/public/---dgreports/---dcomm/---publ/documents/publication/wcms_166021.pdf, p viii

Is the Rise in Unemployment Reversible?

Among the plights of the economic crisis is the contraction in production, both in the industry, and in the overblown services sector. This occurs due to contraction in the market, in foreign trade, private consumption, and in the global stock markets. Job cuts are expected not only in the private sector, but also in the public sector, primarily because governments are driven into implementing emergency plans, part of which means cutting expenses and diminishing the workforce among civil servants.

The current global crisis is nothing like traditional cycles of economic and financial activity, which has always been characterized by crises and recoveries. The continued advancement of humanity toward a single, global system, toward a network of increasingly tighter connections in economy and in society, and toward complete interdependence is an unavoidable process of change. If we can adjust our relations, including our economy and society, to the changes happening in the global-integral world, we will be able to obtain equilibrium with the laws of the new system. That new balance has many advantages to us, yet we currently perceive some of them as negative, even disastrous. Among the most conspicuous of those trends that we perceive as negative is the permanent decline in employment.

The decline in consumption is not transient, nor is the contraction in industrial activity and output. They are both obligatory and reflect a return to reason after an age of over-consumption and its resulting damage. The failing current global economy, with all its competitiveness, egoism, and intrigues, will return to its natural size: a balanced economy. The contraction of industry, services, trade, and the public sector are also mandatory.

All of the economic systems that have spun out of control over the last 30 years, the era of the rule of extreme neo-liberalism, will return to their natural sizes, that are required to provide for the needs of the human race on reasonable, equal, just, and harmonious levels.

In the 2011 Lindau Nobel Laureate Meeting in Economic Sciences, Dr. Joseph E. Stiglitz gave an insightful lecture, titled, "Imagining an Economics that Works: Crisis, Contagion and the Need for a New Paradigm."[81] Near the 15-minute mark of the lecture, Dr. Stiglitz made the following comment: "Today, about 3% of the population is engaged ... in agriculture in the advanced industrial countries, and they produce more food than even an obese society can consume."

Evidently, there is no need for an employment rate of 90%, nor even of 50%. 20% employment is more than enough to cover all essential needs in agriculture, industry, and services of the human society. In other words, the current trend of growing unemployment is not a passing phase, but a new phase humanity is entering.

As we can see, humanity's return to reasonable consumption means that hundreds of millions all over the world will be permanently out of work. If we adopt the suggested program for educating the unemployed, that change will be a welcome one. It will enable us to accelerate the shift in our interrelations to match the global and connected world that humanity has become, where everyone is dependent on everyone else in every aspect of life.

If we do not properly address the challenge of mass global unemployment, it could undermine and topple governments and regimes, creating a worldwide catastrophe.

---

81   "Short films from the 2011 Lindau Nobel Laureate Meeting in Economic Sciences," *The New Palgrave Dictionary of Economics Online*, http://www.dictionaryofeconomics.com/resources/news_lindau_meeting

UNEMPLOYMENT IS HIGHER THAN REPORTED

The true numbers of unemployed in the U.S. and Europe are far higher than reported. The current method of measuring unemployment excludes people who aren't seeking work by their own volition, or who have given up on re-entering the job market. The fact that these people are not counted in the workforce significantly decreases the reported unemployment rate, which is defined as the ratio between the workforce and the general population at working age (usually ages 16-64).

In most countries, even a person who works part time, even an hour a week, is considered employed. There are many other misrepresentations in the current measurements of unemployment, and the majority of those methods tilt the numbers downward. The difference between the reported unemployment and the real one varies among countries, but it would not be an overstatement to say that the actual rates of unemployment are 25%-50% higher than reported.

The contraction of the economic activity due to the global crisis, and the return to balanced economy, are worsening the job crisis. Unemployment is currently a global epidemic expected to keep spreading rapidly, reaching unprecedented proportions. It is a social time bomb whose short fuse has been lit.

UNEMPLOYMENT THREATENS THE STABILITY OF GOVERNMENTS AND REGIMES

It seems as if the rise in unemployment rates worries governments and decision-makers because they fear it is launching social and economic unrest. The state strives to put the unemployed back to work as quickly as possible and is willing to pay the unemployed a basic ration for a limited period of time. Yet no one among decision-makers seems to be asking, "What should a citizen's healthy and balanced life in my county be like? Is it right to encourage unemployed people to rush to find a new job and get back in the (rat) race? Who gains or profits because of it?"

Another point is that dissatisfied citizens will not vote for the party in power, which politicians know all too well. Third, there is genuine fear that the demonstrations and (currently peaceful) protests will become a violent wave, washing over the entire world, as it already has in some Arab world countries. We have already seen sparks of riots, racism, and other forms of violent protests in France, the U.K., Italy, and Greece.

With the Arab Spring in the background, rulers being overthrown, and civil wars and bloodshed breaking out, the tenacity of unemployment is a cause for grave concern for governments and for economists in the Western countries.

AN EMERGENCY PROGRAM TO DEAL WITH UNEMPLOYMENT

As we have seen, rising unemployment and bearish forecasts have created a problem that requires immediate attention. Even countries where the economy is currently solid would do well to adopt the programs presented in this chapter. The interdependence of economies and financial markets throughout the world leaves little doubt that the crisis will spread and affect everyone. Germany, for example, is tied to the Eurozone by its navel. This country is already being hurt by the current financial crisis in Europe, and the prospect of recovery in the near future seems very slim at the moment.

Everyone should recognize that in a closed global and integral system, in a global village, one's fate depends on one's approach toward others. Relations based on mutual concern, social solidarity, balanced consumption, cooperation, and harmony are all mandatory today. The chaotic, volatile reality of our time calls for a change in the awareness of everyone in the world. We must all learn to live in the new network of connections. We must know how to adapt ourselves to it, or we will remain essentially opposite to it, and as long as the gap between us and the network remains, the crisis will keep worsening personally, socially, and globally.

THE PURPOSE OF THE EMERGENCY MECHANISM FOR DEALING WITH UNEMPLOYMENT

To deal with the problem of unemployment, we must set up an emergency mechanism whose goals are as follows:

- Admit the unemployed into a regular study framework (details below), which will be defined as "employment." Anyone who participates in it will not be considered unemployed, either in the state's statistics or in one's social status.
- A participant in the study framework will be given a grant that allows for reasonable sustenance as long as they participate in the program. The term, "unemployment compensation," which is sometimes considered derogatory, will be replaced by "grant" or "scholarship," which testify to the fact that that person is taking part in an educational course. The semantics here are of paramount importance.
- The sum of the grant will be determined by the state, considering the necessities of the employee and his or her family, with the aim of allowing them reasonable provision.
- Another important goal is the prevention of unemployment, bitterness, and mass demonstrations. Just as one's ordinary job forms a social framework, the new educational program will also be a social framework. This framework will alleviate not only social and financial distress, but will also secure a healthy daily schedule, and prevent idleness or decline into crime and various addictions. One who participates in the educational framework in return

for a government sustenance grant will be regarded as "one who has found a job." That person's work is to study and acquire life skills—understanding the new reality and the changes one is committed to undergo to sustain oneself with dignity, as well as to evolve personally and socially toward life in mutual guarantee among all people. A worker who upgrades his personal worth, receives a grant, and feels that the state cares for his or her fate is highly unlikely to go into the streets to demonstrate.

- Provision of practical tools for rejoining the workforce (details below).
- Upgrading the social status of the unemployed from that of an outcast to that of a person entering a process of positive transformation and expansion of social and professional skills.
- Deepening sympathy with the state and social cohesion, even—if not especially—in times of crisis. Understanding the crisis and its causes will prevent arguments and disputes, enhance social cohesion and empathy with the state's institutions, and create a dynamic of change from a sense of sympathy and understanding of the required change on all levels of life.

THE CURRICULUM OF THE EDUCATIONAL PROGRAM

The content of the permanent study framework for unemployed that were "hired" to study in it will be as follows:

- Personal finance, allowing dignified living within the means that the grant provides. Because imbalance of the family budget is a global phenomenon, the antidote is to adopt a routine that will allow people to lead a life of dignity, according to one's financial possibilities. Such courses already exist and have proven themselves successful.

- Studying life skills under conditions of uncertainty, such as maintaining family integrity, parenthood, mental soundness, and improving social skills. The student will also acquire tools to assist one's functioning in the proximate economic surroundings, emphasizing the ramifications of the crisis on one's personal life, social environment, and the values by which one lives.

- Each person will have to understand that in the global world, all of us—ordinary people, policy makers, and tycoons—are in the same boat. Teachings will include explanations of the reasons for the global crisis, its impact on our lives, understanding the interconnections and the irreversible interdependence among individuals, firms, and countries in the entire international system, and the changes incumbent upon us in terms of human relations— the way we communicate, cooperate, and function on the daily level.

- Acquiring the necessary social skills for a stable and peaceful life in the global and interconnected world: social solidarity, consideration of others and of the environment, balanced consumption and so forth. This part of the course will also include an explanation of the necessary transformation in social and economic frameworks of business entities, work places, education systems, and family life. The educational, informational framework will lay down the basis for an internal change. This will be followed by people transforming human relations and internalizing the extent to

which reality has become global and integral. The transformation will include a shift from relations based on competition, individualism, egoism, and maximizing personal benefit, to the kind of relations necessary for mutual dependence among all parts of the system—cooperation, mutual concern, consideration of others' needs, balanced consumption, and mutual guarantee.
- Qualifying students of the educational framework as instructors for newcomers into the framework.

All content will be taught through social activities, simulations, group work, games, and multimedia content. The learning will not be the traditional teacher-class frontal approach.

BENEFITS TO THE STATE FROM THE PROGRAM
DEALING WITH UNEMPLOYMENT
- Systemic and government stability. The government will not be perceived by people as indifferent or as doing only the necessary minimum, but as an entity that regards unemployment as a high-priority issue and allocates substantial resources for that purpose, primarily in developing human capital and people's social skills.
- Enhancing personal empathy with the state and lifting the national morale. Within a few months after the implementation of the program, a new generation will emerge that does not seek riots or unrest. These individuals will know the reason for the crisis and why they lost their jobs. They will also understand the laws of the global and connected world, and the changes incumbent upon each person, and upon society as a whole.

- Optimism is a mighty power. The recognition that we must achieve a balanced economy—not one based on consumerism, but on rational consumption and mutual guarantee—holds within it an optimistic economic and social vision. A generation with such a view will be in a better position to achieve economic prosperity, political and social achievements, thriving health, and a sound family life. This optimism will also allow the state to provide sustainable solutions to the crisis without panic, thus preventing hasty, rash decisions.

- Saving up on resources. Financing the new educational program, paying for grants to the workers, and defining the study as a job will indeed cost money, but will also save a lot of money and resources. Many governments invest in national infrastructure projects and execute large-scale construction projects during crises. The funds spent on the national infrastructure are regarded as "growth-generating investments," and numerous people are employed in executing them. The cost of investment in infrastructures, such as roads and railroads, is far higher than the cost of the emergency program we are suggesting. Moreover, investing in infrastructure will not solve the real problems that today's global and connected world presents. The damages of hidden unemployment—both in the private sector and especially in the public sector—are enormous. The public sector is expected to contract substantially, particularly in Europe, but also in the U.S., and taking the unemployed into the new education-

and-grant program will be far less expensive, and far more efficient, than employing them in national projects.

- Financing the efforts to deal with the unemployment problem: The cost of employing a person in the public sector in most countries is overblown and entails large-scale hidden unemployment. The salary of a person who is actually in hidden unemployment can finance the grants of at least two unemployed persons. The expected growth in unemployment and cuts will save the money that will be invested in establishing and maintaining the government educational framework. This will qualify those who were ejected from the job market, and ease their transition into the new way of life.
- For more details on the surplus following the expected rise in unemployment, see Chapter, "Surplus and Improving the Public's Well-Being."

THE PROGRAM'S BENEFITS TO THE UNEMPLOYED

Immediate implementation of the program holds great benefits to those who have lost their jobs, starting with the ability to provide for one's family, through acquiring life-skills and tools for managing the family budget, improvement of the social status and self-esteem, and acquiring knowledge and social skills necessary for any person in today's global and interdependent world. Understanding "the big picture," that we belong to an educational framework that equips every person with the tools to become integrated in the new world, along with a supportive social environment, will give hope and optimism for the future. At the same time, it will create a way of life that has a better balance between work (study), family, community, and society.

DEFUSING THE SOCIAL TIME-BOMB

At the end of the day, it is hard for us to come to terms with the fact that unemployment has not yet peaked, but is expected to climb to unprecedented proportions. The current economic and social systems will not be able to cope with the ramifications of unemployment in the high double digits; thus, the suggested program will allow both citizens and state to mutually adjust to the new situation. The unique curricula will prevent unrest and violence. It will allow for normal life to continue as one proceeds toward a transformation in human relations, in keeping with the new interdependence revealed by the current crisis. That change will result in a new, balanced economy under the umbrella of mutual guarantee, which will facilitate not only the provision of people's basic needs, but also a better quality of life, profound fulfillment, harmony, and sustainable social and economic structures.

Looking forward, it is likely that many will choose to join the program, regardless of circumstances. Some will even choose it as a way of life. The surplus in productivity and technological progress, along with the return to a balanced and reasonable economy, will ease the transition to a dignified existence for all the people in the world, assuming the majority of them will choose to live under the principles taught at the educational program.

A few will provide agricultural products, a few will provide industrial goods, and a few will provide the services and trade necessary for our lives. It will be possible to alternate performing those functions, as long as the focus is not on material goods and competition. Instead, the focus will be on personal and social development, and strengthening ties of mutual guarantee and harmony among all people, and between humanity and Nature.

THE PSYCHOLOGY OF ECONOMICS

APPRECIATION OF THE SOCIAL ENVIRONMENT AND SATISFACTION FROM GIVING WILL "FUEL" THE ECONOMY OF MUTUAL GUARANTEE

Key Points
- Human beings aspire to enjoy as much as possible with the least possible effort.
- Behavioral economics combines psychological and social considerations in predicting economic behavior.
- Every person is strongly affected by society, even by those of whom we are not aware. We appreciate ourselves compared to those in our environment, and cannot tolerate having less than others around us.
- In the current social and economic frameworks, people cannot be satisfied, nor can society continue to remain stable.
- The new society that will thrive by relying on relative and idiosyncratic equality. Those within it will be rewarded with the fulfillment of psychological needs that they are not expressing today.

- A mutual guarantee-based economy will have altruistic characteristics.

Every scientific method begins with a premise, and economics is no exception to the rule. While hard sciences engage in minerals, plants, and the cosmos at large, economics engages in something far more volatile and unpredictable: human nature. One such premise in economics is John Stuart Mill's[82] "homo economicus" (the economic human). Roughly speaking, the goal of the economic human, namely each of us, is to obtain the maximum pleasure for the least effort.

And what does the economic human enjoy? The consumption of goods. The more goods we consume, the more we enjoy our lives. Additionally, we are not keen on hard work, so we weigh everything by the measure of exertion required to obtain our goods. Economic humans wish to maximize their benefits by choosing the alternative that best serves their preferences under their budget limitations.

BEHAVIORAL ECONOMICS: MONEY ISN'T EVERYTHING

Until recently, economists asserted that utility could be measured by material possessions. That is, the more we consume, the more we enjoy. This approach has led to our current state, in which the attainment of money is the ultimate gauge of success.

According to this approach, man is a rational being—a key concept in economics. A rational person will weigh all the options and finally choose the most rewarding in terms of material resources, money, or products that can be measured monetarily. Thus, we have developed a societal view that money provides a gauge with which to measure a person.

However, researchers in behavioral economics have shown that people take many other elements into account besides

---

82 "John Stuart Mill," Primary Contributor: Richard Paul Anschutz, *Encyclopedia Britannica*, http://www.britannica.com/EBchecked/topic/382623/John-Stuart-Mill

money when making decisions. One such example can be found in a well-known experiment in behavioral economics, called the "Ultimatum Game."[83] In this experiment, two participants must share a sum of money between them, say 100 dollars. The first participant offers the second one part of the sum, and if the second participant agrees, they divide the money accordingly. If not, neither gets a penny.

If, indeed, money were the only element taken into account, the second participant would have agreed to receive whatever was offered, even one dollar, while the other party received the rest, since the receiver would have had one dollar more than before. However, in many cases, the participants agreed only on equal distribution, and were willing to relinquish much more than one dollar if they felt that the initial offer was unjust.

THE STUDY OF HAPPINESS

Eyal Winter, Professor of Economics at the Hebrew University of Jerusalem, explains that while it is clear that man should aspire to economic welfare, often defined as "well-being," classical economics assumes that a person strives to maximize material gains because for most of human history, economic success was required for survival.[84] As a result, a mechanism evolved within us that compels us to obtain the means to survive, which is expressed in money.

However, researchers of positive psychology, Prof. Ed Diener and Robert Biswas-Diener, PhD, summarized dozens of studies and found that, "There are mostly small correlations between income and subjective well-being (SWB) ... although these correlations appear to be larger in poor nations." Moreover, "People who prize material goals more than other values tend to be substantially less happy, unless they are rich. Thus, more money may enhance SWB

---

83   http://en.wikipedia.org/wiki/Ultimatum_game
84   http://www.ma.huji.ac.il/~mseyal/

when it means avoiding poverty and living in a developed nation, but income appears to increase SWB little over the long-term when more of it is gained by well-off individuals whose material desires rise with their incomes."[85]

Another interesting study, "Lottery Winners and Accident Victims: Is Happiness Relative?"[86] compared the level of happiness among lottery winners and people who became handicapped by accidents. It found that approximately a year after the event, a person who won the lottery was not happier than a person who was crippled by a tragic accident.

THE SATISFACTION FROM GIVING, COOPERATION, AND FAIRNESS

While material well-being has evolved as a basic need, many other needs have developed in us over thousands of years of living in social frameworks. One such primary need that formed from leading a social life is the need to give and to receive. Human societies have always worked in cooperation because it enhanced their sustainability. Cavemen were far more successful in hunting and protecting themselves and their clans when they collaborated and lived a communal life. An individual who did not cooperate risked being ostracized, which often meant certain death.

The tendency to cooperate to achieve satisfaction still exists within us as strongly as the mechanism that assures our material well-being. An often-played game in behavioral economics is known as "The Dictator Game." In it, a player receives a sum of money and is supposed to decide how much of it to keep. Approximately 80% of players give some money to the other player, and about 20% of those split the sum evenly.[87] This demonstrates how giving, cooperation, and fairness bring us

---

85   http://www.intentionalhappiness.com/articles/July-2009/Money-Happiness-2002.pdf
86   Brickman, Philip; Coates, Dan; Janoff-Bulman, Ronnie, "Lottery winners and accident victims: Is happiness relative?" *Journal of Personality and Social Psychology*, Vol 36(8), Aug 1978, 917-927, http://psycnet.apa.org/index.cfm?fa=buy.optionToBuy&id=1980-01001-001
87   http://en.wikipedia.org/wiki/Dictator_game

more satisfaction than the satisfaction that comes simply by receiving money.

SOCIAL INFLUENCE

People measure themselves in relation to their social environment. They then make decisions based on emotions that arise during one's social relations. In a study of participants in the above "Ultimatum Game," the participants' brain activity was monitored while deciding whether to take the amount of money offered. It turned out that in the process of receiving the offer, two different areas were working in the brain—the area in charge of making rational decisions, and the area in charge of anger.

The more unfair the participant considered the offer, the more the activity of the anger segment of the brain prevailed over the rational consideration. The participant tended to reject the offer and remain without the money.

One always compares oneself to others in their reference group. Because our social nature causes this behavior, emotions of contentment and satisfaction—or indifference, frustration, and anger—join rational considerations. These responses result from our social relations, and may lead us to make choices that yield negative results, both toward us and toward society.

This was demonstrated in many studies, such as that of Professors Sara Solnick and David Hemenway, "Are Positional Concerns Stronger in Some Domains than in Others?" In their study, they claim, "Given a constant purchasing power of money, almost half of respondents would prefer to live in a poorer world, earning $200,000 rather than $400,000, if most other people were earning $100,000 rather than $800,000."

However, the combination of comparing ourselves with others, along with the influence of the environment, can also bring positive results. On April 8, 2011, Justina Wheale of *The*

Epoch Times wrote, "In a new study published in the *Journal of Personality and Social Psychology*, Dr. Karl Aquino and his team found that after witnessing exceptionally altruistic acts, people are more likely to perform charitably themselves."[88]

Dr. Aquino and his team also wrote, "They have some sort of emotional reaction—they're inspired, they feel somewhat awed by the behavior, they may get severe physiological reactions. A lot of these changes can then lead them to try to do good things for others."

EMOTIONAL CONTAGION

We affect each other in more ways than we realize. Our influence on one another is not only what we see and measure in others—studies show that we "emotionally infect" one another, and are "infected" by them even without noticing it. Beyond the fact that we assess people's expressions and deduce their emotional states, there are cells in our brains called "mirror neurons," which respond to other people's actions by activating the same areas in our own brains, as if we were performing that same action.

But are we influenced only by the people we meet? It turns out that we are influenced by people we don't even know. In the book, *Connected: The Surprising Power of Our Social Networks and How They Shape Our Lives—How Your Friends' Friends' Friends Affect Everything You Feel, Think, and Do*, Dr. Nicholas A. Christakis and Prof. James Fowler introduce the concept that every human being is meshed in social interconnections and networks. According to Christakis and Fowler, important aspects in our lives are influenced by people up to three degrees of remoteness from us, even if we don't know them personally.

"Our own research has shown that the spread of influence in social networks obeys what we call the Three Degrees of

88   Justina Wheale, "Witnessing Acts of Compassion Prompts People to Do Good," *The Epoch Times* (April 8, 2011), http://www.theepochtimes.com/n2/science/witnessing-acts-of-compassion-prompts-people-to-do-good-study-54278.html

Influence Rule. Everything we do or say tends to ripple through our network, having an impact on our friends (one degree), our friends' friends (two degrees), and even our friends' friends' friends (three degrees). ...Likewise, we are influenced by friends within three degrees."[89] Our health, wealth, and indeed happiness are largely a function of what people three degrees of remoteness from us think and do.

THE CRISIS AND THE INFLUENCE OF THE SOCIAL ENVIRONMENT

These connections become more complicated and more prominent as the world becomes increasingly globalized. The tightening connections among the various parts of the world have turned the human society into a single global and integral system, causing every element to become dependent on every other element in the system.

Lecturers in happiness economics often ask their audiences to find out where their clothes and gadgets were made, thus demonstrating how dependent we are on other countries in the world. But the connection between all of us is far broader and deeper than our clothes or smart-phones.

In his depiction of the modern world, economist Geoff Mulgan wrote, "The starting point for understanding the world today is not the size of its GDP or the destructive power of its weapons systems, but the fact that it is so much more joined together than before. It may look like it is made up of separate and sovereign individuals, firms, nations or cities, but the deeper reality is one of multiple connections."[90]

Under such conditions, the traditional economy, which is based on individualism, isn't working any longer, and today's global crisis is proving it each day. It is impossible to pursue

---

89 Nicholas A. Christakis and James Fowler, *Connected: The Surprising Power of Our Social Networks and How They Shape Our Lives—How Your Friends' Friends' Friends Affect Everything You Feel, Think, and Do* (NY: Back Bay Books, 2011), 26
90 Mulgan, Geoff, *Connexity: Responsibility, Freedom, Business and Power in the New Century* (revised edn.) (London: Viking, 1998), 3

personal gain without including the myriad connections that affect each and every one of us.

In 1996, renowned sociologist, Manuel Castells, argued persuasively that "...a new economy emerged around the world."[91] We can use the changes that the economic system is undergoing to balance our material needs with our social needs. However, when we examine today's society, we see that seeking material benefits and personal gain are disproportionally more dominant in society and in the media than ever before. This is a manifestation of consumption that has grown out of control.

An average person in the U.S. is exposed to approximately 600 commercials daily, all carefully crafted to convince us that the satisfaction and benefits from buying the advertised product will make us happy.[92]

In truth, the only satisfaction obtained is the advertisers'. Also, we are often promised rewards for personal success, even when that success may come at the expense of others. It follows that a person will do the utmost to gain and feel superior to others.

We live in this world buffeted by two conflicting influences. We are fast becoming aware that we are unable to provide for all of our own needs, and need to depend on others, who in turn depend on us in the same way. The media, however, relentlessly pitches to us the idea that the more each of us possesses, the more successful and superior we are to others. These messages surround us, although by now it is quite clear that we are not self-sufficient and that wealth is not the only means of achieving happiness.

---

91   Castells, Manuel, "Information technology and global capitalism" in W. Hutton and A. Giddens. (eds.) *On The Edge. Living with global capitalism* (London: Vintage, 2001), 52
92   "Our Rising Ad Dosage, It's Not as Oppressive as Some Think," *Media Matters* (February 15, 2007), p 2, https://www.mediadynamicsinc.com/UserFiles/File/MM_Archives/Media%20Matters%2021507.pdf

On the one hand, since we always compare ourselves to others, when one person has more than others, it arouses envy and makes others wish that person to fail. On the other hand, attempts at communism, where everyone has the same amount, have failed bitterly. In the Soviet Union "experiment" with communism, the coercive leveling of people's material assets, regardless of individual needs and without proper education and explanation—necessary components of voluntary change—resulted in the death of tens of millions.

This led to the ultimate demise of the regime and an enduring aura of negativity around the entire idea of this philosophy. Forced solutions do not work, especially when they radically differ from those preceding them. We should carefully heed that lesson now that humanity has reached a tipping point in its evolution and is beginning to move from the failed, contemporary economy into a new, balanced economy connected by the concept of mutual guarantee.

We cannot detach ourselves from society, as it provides us with all that we need for life. Accordingly, any paradigm or attempt to solve the global crisis with tools from the old economy is bound to fail, as such attempts derive from a competitive, self-centered approach that is quickly becoming obsolete. Instead of trying to "force" our existing models on reality, we should try to change the economic system and human society to match the newly emerging reality.

Essentially, we are referring to a psychological transformation. Just as humans developed mechanisms that assist us in coping with the elements, today we can adapt our thinking to become congruent with the conditions of the 21st century.

SOCIAL JUSTICE AND EQUALITY

Sociologist Ulrich Beck wrote in his book, *Brave New World of Work*, that in the new society, people will conduct "civil labor" to benefit society. Yet, how can such a society bring satisfaction and a sense of fulfillment to people?

The new society must recognize that if we measure ourselves in relation to others, we will never feel satisfied or believe that we have obtained social justice. A society that wishes to exist in peace and prosperity must ensure that each person has the possibility of leading a full and balanced life, liberated from the need to worry about providing for staples and bare necessities. As described above, material well-being can bring only a certain level of happiness, and society neither should, nor can equalize everyone financially. Rather, there should be distribution based on an equality in which each receives according to one's *unique* needs for a reasonable, dignified existence.

Such a "normative" standard of living will be determined as one that is guaranteed for every person—mutual guarantee. That is, the standard of living must be higher than the poverty line and defined in a collaborative process through a "round table" form of deliberation. Equality among people will be expressed not so much in the amount of goods or funds allotted each person, but more in the fairness of the distribution and its transparency.

Moreover, the sense of equality among people will be expressed by everyone having the ability to obtain complete self-realization and personal fulfillment. People will also share the awareness that the mechanism of mutual guarantee is what creates the equality and the so-needed sense of fairness. This sense will exist at every level of human relations: interpersonal, between person and state, and between the economic paradigm and the social one.

LOOKING AHEAD—A CHANGE WE CAN MAKE

This mechanism of mutual guarantee will diminish and ultimately eliminate social gaps. The guaranteeing of people's basic needs for a reasonable existence is the key difference between an economy of mutual guarantee and the current economics. We have already seen that individuals have many needs that cannot be met in an environment that does not encourage their expression and fulfillment. The more the social environment presents models of the joy that exists in social relations, in sharing, and in fairness, the more individuals will be able to enjoy life in a society where such relationships are the norm. This is the key to the change.

As Dr. Aquino is quoted in the above-mentioned publication in *The Epoch Times*, "We suggest an alternative technique may be to highlight examples of extraordinary goodness. They're rare by definition; they don't happen every day. But if we could identify these and make them much more prominent, then it could get people to think differently about their lives and about others, which may influence them to do good."

Indeed, there are ways to emphasize acts of altruism and to see how the change affects each of us. For example, if a list of the 100 people who contributed the most to society were to constantly be advertised, we would see how the same abilities that led people to gain while exploiting others will now lead them to work for the good of society. The same competitive drive that makes us want to succeed at others' expense will now lead us to realize our potential to win the respect and esteem of society. In addition, the closer personal interest and social benefit become, the more a person will be granted social and public support to actualize his or her best.

The new "fuel" will change our nature from materialistic and egoistic to altruistic and prosocial. Appreciating our environment and gaining satisfaction by giving are the keys to our choosing to live our lives within an economic and social system of mutual guarantee.

There is a twofold benefit in that change: activity to benefit society will yield a society that exists in peace and prosperity, providing a supportive environment to all its members. Additionally, individuals will be able to fully realize their personal potentials and goals, thus gaining both personal satisfaction and public appreciation.

In the current chaotic environment, such a vision may seem vague or unreal, but even striving for mutual guarantee will make it clear that all it takes to achieve this is a psychological shift of mindset.

TYCOONS IN THE NEW ECONOMY

FROM PREDATORS TO PROSOCIAL—
THE POSITIVE ROLE OF TYCOONS
IN THE NEW ECONOMY

Key Points

- Currently, 1% of the world's population holds 40% of the world's wealth.
- The vast social and economic gaps evoke in many a sense of injustice.
- Frustration and protests are aimed toward tycoons, who are perceived as having gained their riches at the expense of the public by manipulating the system.
- A wealthy individual is entitled to enjoy the fruits of his or her work. We have no moral justification to force tycoons into contributing financially to society.
- Tycoons provide work for a great many people. Hurting them will hurt their employees.

- People are not born equal in their talents or abilities. The equality required in the global-integral system is a relative and idiosyncratic one where each person receives according to the needs and according to the contribution to society.
- Through education and the influence of the social environment toward mutual guarantee, tycoons will join in with the new economy and contribute their skills to the well-being of all. In return, they will enjoy social approbation and a sense of fulfillment.

The world's social unrest and the demand for social justice bring out prolonged frustration, particularly among the middle class and the less affluent portions of society. These classes bear most of the burden for the global rise in the cost of living and growing inequality.

The current economic crisis is aggravating this class distress and this is primarily seen in the PIIGS countries in Europe and also in the U.S., although protests have also erupted in economies whose growth seems currently solid, such as Israel and even Germany.

In a globalized and interconnected world, even countries that enjoy a robust economy are affected by the crisis, and there is tangible dependence and mutual influence among markets. Another issue is that the fruits of economic growth have not been evenly distributed, so the economic and social gaps have grown significantly in recent years. Millions of people are being pushed below the poverty line[93] and even into hunger,[94] with the middle class bearing the lion's share of the tax burden, working harder than ever to make ends meet.

The erosion of wages in the middle classes is pressuring families in both middle and lower classes, creating widespread

---

93   By: Associated Press, "Number of US "poor" reaches record high under new census formula," *The Guardian* (November 7, 2011), http://www.guardian.co.uk/society/2011/nov/07/us-poverty-census-formula

94   "Hunger in America: 2012 United States Hunger and Poverty Facts," *Hunger Notes*, http://www.worldhunger.org/articles/Learn/us_hunger_facts.htm

resentment by the majority of people, usually referred to as "the 99 percent." That resentment is turned primarily against governments and policy-makers, who are perpetuating the current economic system that has brought them into this hardship. Primarily, criticism is aimed at the financial industry, which plays a leading role in the global crisis, and toward the centralization of the market in the hands of a few super-wealthy individuals, known as "tycoons."

A "tycoon" is an informal name for a business magnate—one who has reached prominence and derived a notable amount of wealth from a particular industry, such as banking, oil, or high-tech. In some cases, tycoons are dominant in more than one industry. The word, "tycoon," derives from the Japanese word *taikun*, which means "great lord," and was used as a title for a shogun (a Japanese military ruler). The word was first used in English in 1857.[95]

Interestingly, according to Adam Goodheart, author of *1861: The Civil War Awakening*, "Abraham Lincoln's secretaries, John Hay and John Nicolay, used ... a nickname for their boss behind his back: 'The Tycoon.'"[96] Since then, the term has spread to the business community, where it has been in use ever since.

1% OF THE WORLD'S POPULATION HOLDS 40% OF THE WORLD'S WEALTH

One of the reasons why anger is turned against tycoons is the disproportionate level of centralization of wealth. Currently, 1% of the world's population holds 40% of the world's wealth.[97] Such extreme centralization affects the stability of the financial

---

95   http://www.merriam-webster.com/dictionary/tycoon
96   Adam Goodheart, "Return of the Samurai," *The New York Times* (November 10, 2010), http://opinionator.blogs.nytimes.com/2010/11/10/return-of-the-samurai/
97   "40% of world's wealth owned by 1% of population," *CBCNews* (December 5, 2006), http://www.cbc.ca/news/business/story/2006/12/05/globalwealth.html, James Randerson, "World's richest 1% own 40% of all wealth, UN report discovers," *The Guardian* (December 6, 2006), http://www.guardian.co.uk/money/2006/dec/06/business. internationalnews

system and economic activity throughout the market, since the dominance of the firms owned by the tycoons affects public welfare, which is subject to ties and interests of the dominant firms, their strategies, and the priorities of a ruling few.

A study[98] conducted by S. Vitali, J.B. Glattfelder, and S. Battiston of the Swiss Federal Institute of Technology tested the links of 43,000 international corporations. The study located a relatively small group of firms, primarily banks that hold a disproportionate share of the global economy. The study, "The Network of Global Corporate Control," found 1318 companies that had ties to two or more other companies. At the core of the network, the study found, members averaged "ties to 20 other members. As a result, about 3/4 of the ownership of firms in the core remains in the hands of firms of the core itself."[99] Through their shares, the 1318 companies collectively held the majority of production and technology companies, which represent 60% of the global income.

In recent years, the growth engines of those companies have been to acquire even more companies, resulting in perpetually growing corporations. At the head of the pyramid is a tycoon, who usually owns 20-30 companies, and whose favor is sought by banks and other financial institutions. Thus, the system supports tycoons and encourages them to keep growing.

The economics of scale that helps tycoons reduce their costs also helps them when competing with smaller businesses. By pushing smaller companies and manufacturers out of business, tycoons not only grow more, but increase their per-unit profit because now they can drive up their prices, undaunted by competition.

But can tycoons really be blamed for their behavior? In an environment of untamed and ruthless competition, their choice

98   S. Vitali, J.B. Glattfelder, and S. Battiston, "The Network of Global Corporate Control," Swiss Federal Institute of Technology (arXiv:1107.5728v1 [q-fin.GN], 28 Jul 2011)
99   Ibid, p 5

(if they want to play in the market) is to either be hunters or hunted. Yet, instead of blaming the system, we blame those who use it best, forgetting that their skills and resourcefulness could be used favorably if only the economic system encouraged collaboration instead of competition. When you have a person at the top of the pyramid, be it a tycoon or a president, it is easier to put the blame on them rather than mend the system that created them.

For the sake of argument, let us assume that two babies are born on the same day, one to a king, and one to the king's gardener. Can you blame them for being born into their respective families? Each person has a different starting point in life, not only in wealth, but also in schooling, environment, and so on. How can one determine which of them is more successful? There are people who succeed because of an inheritance that they received, or who came into their fortunes on their own. Here, too, fate plays a part.

As long as one's means of gaining wealth is within the accepted norms of that person's society, there is no moral justification to demand that the person share his or her fortune or relinquish it. It is impossible to demand social justice by forcing the wealthy to donate more than others, provided they have paid the taxes they must pay by law. You can increase their taxes or regulate the centralization, but there is a long way between constitutional changes and regulations, and stripping the wealth from the rich.

THE CRITICISM IS NOT WITHOUT MERIT

The criticism of tycoons reflects the criticism of the extremes to which capitalism has been taken—cultivating consumerism and extreme inequality, and compelling us to lead a life of stress, debt, and constant pressure as we pursue a never-achieved happiness from acquiring material possessions. Studies indicate that people who focus on materialism tend to suffer from high levels of anxiety and depression.[100]

Meanwhile, tycoons have become a symbol of inequality; they are regarded as one of the causes of the perpetuation of the existing system. Neo-liberalism, which idealized individualism, free competition, and diminishing government intervention to the minimum possible, is what allows tycoons to use their natural gifts and increase their power and wealth.

Tycoons do not hesitate to act to maximize their personal benefit, but when a billionaire employs tens of thousand of workers at minimum wages, or subcontracts work to a factory in East Asia that employs people under slavery conditions, it arouses antagonism. The companies owned by tycoons are not altruistic entities. The degree to which capitalism has evolved gives them permission and incentives to do all that they can to increase their profits, often exploiting their monopolistic power to spike prices and maximize profits. As is well known, those who are hurt the most by this policy are the lower economic classes.

Also, as reported in the above-mentioned "The Network of Global Corporate Control" report, "Many of the top actors belong to the core. This means that they do not carry out their business in isolation. On the contrary, they are tied together in an extremely entangled web of control."[101] This web of control allows tycoons to bind customers to them through engagements that exploit these customers. Moreover, they often use their ties to government institutions to promote their special interests by employing lobbyists. Although greed is not unique to tycoons, they have more tools to realize it than others, with subsequently more adverse effects on society and the environment.

The global crisis hurt the business world in general and tycoons in particular. The majority of their activities are heavily leveraged, having been financed with credit received from

100   Kasser, Tim, *The High Price of Materialism* Cambridge, (U.S.A., MIT Press, Oct 1, 2003)
101   Vitali, Glattfelder, and Battiston, "The Network of Global Corporate Control," p 32

banks or institutional investors. When a business that tycoons purchase with credit (loans) cannot meet the debt with which it was bought, tycoons do not hesitate to declare that they will not be able to fully repay their debt, and ask for the banks and institutional investors (where our pension money is invested) to partake in the damage, meaning to write off some of the debt.

In the short range, this process causes great damages to many people, while the tycoons come out relatively unscathed. However, their financial wizardry is costing them heavily, tarnishing their public image and creating public pressure to restrain their power and regulate their actions. Some are heavily engaged in philanthropy, such as Bill Gates through the Bill and Melinda Gates Foundation, but for the most part that activity is perceived as both a disguise and inconsequential compared to their extreme wealth, clout, and the damages they inflict on the economy and the environment.

Finally, the lavish lifestyle that many of the super-rich have adopted arouses envy, or loathing, or both, but leaves no one indifferent.

Unjust Criticism toward Tycoons

There is a degree of dishonesty in the enmity toward tycoons and the desire to see them fall. We love to hate tycoons because we are not tycoons. In all likelihood, if I were a tycoon, I would defend with all my heart the economic and social system that allows for our emergence. For the most part, these are simply successful entrepreneurs. In fact, the American Dream feeds on such rags-to-riches stories, and the hope to achieve that dream is what fuels the entire economic system. We hate tycoons because for them, the American Dream came true, and for us, it has become a nightmare, or at best, remains a dream still to be achieved.

Moreover, striving to destroy the tycoons' businesses can destroy precisely those who fight them the hardest. For all their greed, tycoons provide work for hundreds of thousands of people. If they were to fail, all those whose livelihood depends on them would fail with them. There is merit to the demand of tycoons to sell some of their businesses in order to decrease the centralization of the market, but how will the buyers of these businesses behave? Will they be fairer to the public? Or will they be new tycoons who behave just like the ones from whom they bought the business? In fact, experience shows that sometimes the buyer actually raises prices and cuts jobs more than the previous owner to boost profit, increase returns on the investment and repay the debt with which the purchase was financed.

Indeed, the question of the public's approach toward tycoons has no simple answer.

Interdependence Affects Tycoons, As Well

We can argue about whether or not the system is just, but in fact, the majority of people depend on tycoons for their livelihood. We need to understand that we are all in the same boat and in the same economic system, in which we are all interdependent. Evidently, the current method is not ideal, and manipulations of powerful people and institutions have a lot to do with its faults, but we cannot upend the system altogether. Attempting to create social justice by destroying tycoons will actually destroy the society that destroys them, and the first to suffer will be those who depend on tycoons for their livelihood—nearly all of us— because they'll be out of a job.

In fact, arguing in favor of destroying the tycoons indicates a lack of understanding of the economic system. If, for example, everyone stopped buying in big chain stores such as Walmart and went back to buying at local grocery stores, those mega-stores would fire their workers, who would then have no money to buy at the local grocery stores. In other words, before we demand any changes, we must understand that every system is interlinked.

In a socioeconomic system based on mutual guarantee (where all guarantee each other's well-being), no one will force anyone to relinquish their property or funds. Coercion contradicts the very spirit of mutual guarantee.

If tycoons do not make concessions of their own volition, and the concessions are not supplemented and complemented with education toward norms of mutual guarantee, the existing situation will only deteriorate. A forced solution will hurt our source of income because while that tycoon is getting richer at the expense of numerous workers earning minimum wages, they at least *have* an income. Tycoons and their employees are all tied together; they are codependent. If the tycoons go down, all who depend on them will go down with them.

THE SOLUTION—EVOLUTION, NOT REVOLUTION

While it is tempting to head out to the streets and yell out demands for justice, actually doing so would only worsen the situation. After all, when has destruction led to good results? From the bloody French Revolution through the 1917 Bolshevik Revolution in Russia and up to the 2011 revolution in Egypt, rarely—if ever—has a revolution achieved positive results. While the situation that emerged after the dust settled and the blood dried might have improved aspects of life prior to the revolution, if humanity could *evolve* into better states instead of revolting into them, it would be better for all.

When tycoons feel unsafe, they simply flee to other countries where they are more welcome, as is the case in Russia today.[102,103] This is hardly a desirable scenario. A change for the better can only emerge from reconstructing our relations and the economic and social systems resulting from them. This must be done

102 Harvey Morris, "Russian Oligarchs Flee To Safety In Israel," *The Financial Times - UK* (March 24, 2005), http://www.rense.com/general63/oky.htm
103 Luke Harding, "Mobile phone oligarch flees Russia for new life in Britain," *The Guardian* (January 27, 2009), http://www.guardian.co.uk/world/2009/jan/27/russia-kremlin-oligarchs

by providing information and education. The shift from the current state to a more desirable one must be gradual, without irresponsibly breaking the power of tycoons or of any powerful element in the market.

Because the required shift today is from perceiving ourselves as separate entities to perceiving ourselves as connected elements in a global interdependent system, changing our perception is the only possible solution. A change of perception is a gradual, extended process that requires time for people to absorb and accept. The more we advance into the new perception of the world, the more we will progress toward decentralizing the market and dealing with the rest of the problems in the market. However, this *must* be done with mutual consent, not by force.

EXPLANATION, EDUCATION, AND THE INFLUENCE OF THE ENVIRONMENT

The demonstrations throughout the world calling for social justice, and the damage to the economy and to society from over centralization, inequality, and the unchecked power of tycoons, have pressured governments into acting to reduce the centralization and the influence of tycoons. Traditional means have been tighter regulations, structural changes in the market, additional taxes on the super-rich and on prestigious brands. But given the clout that tycoons have, it is unlikely that such measures will be fully implemented, if at all. Moreover, even if they are implemented, it is unlikely that they will lead to reduction in the cost of living, diminish the social and economic gaps, or ease the sense of social injustice.

Such regulatory measures are instruments from the old toolbox used when the world still consisted of separate entities. In today's world, with the globally connected system where everyone depends on everyone else, instruments that facilitate competition cannot work. The key to a *voluntary* transformation—in consensus, through a round table type discussion, as equals—is provision of information and education to the masses. In an interconnected system, how can one person exploit another? It would be tantamount to self-inflicted harm. When social norms foster mutual consideration, mutual concern, social solidarity, and cohesion, the issue of tycoons will find its peaceful solution in no time.

Such a change is achievable only through expansive provision of information, intelligent use of media, and an education system that enlightens every single person, stresses the importance of mutual guarantee, and gives people motivation to contribute to the best of their ability, whether a magnate or an indigent.

When the desirable change takes place, people will perceive tycoons as parts of themselves. They will recognize the tycoons' contribution to society. On the other hand, the tycoons will begin to behave responsibly toward society and the environment. They will willingly adopt the required changes in the new economic system, changes that include a more equal distribution of financial resources. Such a solution, which is based on transformation in perception through education toward mutual guarantee, is the only solution that is positive and sustainable.

TYCOONS IN THE NEW ECONOMY—THE SHIFT FROM FINANCIAL TYCOONS TO SOCIAL TYCOONS

First, it is important to note that in a mutual guarantee-based system in the global and connected world, tycoons have their rightful place. The equality required in a harmonious society is not absolute equality, but is relative and idiosyncratic, where each receives according to one's needs and contribution to society. If a businessperson frequently travels abroad and needs a private jet to be more mobile and efficient, thus providing his or her many employees with work, than that person should have a jet. In such a case, it is not a luxury but a necessary tool from which the entire society benefits.

In that sense, the tycoon will not sense that financial benefits have been taken away. Quite the contrary, these benefits now have social legitimacy. Even in a society where equality is the highest value, some will excel and earn more. The question is, "What they will earn? Will it be billions in the bank?" We have yet to see that such billions help anyone in the current crisis. Billions in the bank have also not proven to be a guarantee for happiness, but the contrary.

Instead of money, a new motivation will give people a reason to keep active and working, even in a society of relative equality—the appreciation and approval of fellow citizens for the benefits that the tycoons produce for society. Tycoons will be able to realize their personal and business potentials since the majority of them enjoy not only the profits, but view themselves primarily as entrepreneurs, enjoying the action and not just the profit that it yields. In the new society, there will be mechanisms for advertising people's contribution to society and expressing due gratitude, which will guarantee that the entrepreneurs are well rewarded.

Equal distribution of income is not a just act because not all people are the same, with the same needs. If equal distribution were to be implemented, its harm would be greater than its benefit. Equality must remain relative, addressing not only the most fundamental needs of people, but also expressing their unique contributions to society and their efforts to benefit others. People have a natural need to be rewarded for their work—both socially and materially. An equal income will hamper people's motivation to contribute and will cause a drastic rise in depression.

The mutual guarantee economy will bring about a drastic, though voluntary reduction of socioeconomic inequality. Society need not and cannot make everyone equal by arbitrarily dividing up income, services, or material resources. Instead, the solution, as mentioned above, is based on *relative* equality, where one receives according to one's needs.

There will be a minimum standard of living set by the state. That minimum will secure basic provisions and allow for reasonable and dignified living according to one's particular needs or the needs of one's family, and in relation to one's social environment. It will, however, always be a standard of living that is above the poverty line, which will be defined in a joint round-table type discussion. The equality will manifest in fairness of resource distribution and transparency of the system.

When we all live in a society that has made mutual guarantee its prime value, the values of tycoons will change as well, from wanting to control others and maximize their personal gain at the expense of others into prosocial values by contributing to society. The magnates and moguls of society will be appreciated not because of their lavish lifestyles, but because of their contributions to society and to the environment.

Utilizing the skills and abilities of tycoons for society's benefit are what will turn the "social" tycoons into fulfilled and satisfied individuals, just as in a family, where the prime provider enjoys his or her contribution to the sustenance and well-being of the entire family.

A DREAM OR A REALITY?

The harmonious way of life we have described may seem unrealistic and far-fetched, but the global crisis caused by the competitive and individualistic nature of our current way of life, compared to the way we ought to live in our global and connected world, will accelerate the change. And when the change occurs, we will see that our natural reflex to stick to the existing system despite its obvious flaws does not serve our interests, and that we have a chance to build a beautiful, harmonious, and sustainable reality where everyone, even tycoons, have a rightful place.

SURPLUS AND IMPROVING THE PUBLIC'S WELL-BEING

THE MUTUAL GUARANTEE ECONOMY WILL EXPOSE MANY SURPLUSES, WHICH WILL FUND THE CHANGE AHEAD OF US

Key Points

- Over-industrialization, overproduction, and overconsumption have made our modern economy inefficient. Many resources are exploited not for people's well-being, but to maintain the existing system.

- The current economic system is depleting the natural resources necessary for our existence, although there is no real shortage of them. Inconsiderate exploitation of natural resources contradicts the attitude of mutual guarantee (where all are guarantors of each other's well-being), incumbent upon us due to our living in a global-integral world.

- The transition into a balanced and functional economy will expose many financial, material, and social surpluses, which will be diverted toward public benefit as a result of the transformation in our relationships and the adoption of mutual guarantee as a global socioeconomic treaty.
- In realizing the principle of mutual guarantee in society and in the economy, we will discover that the needs of the world society can be met while allowing Earth to replenish its resources and exist in comfort and harmony with humanity and Nature.

A key element in the current economic theory is lack. Among other fields of research, economists study the use of finite resources that can be replaced by others. A lack does not mean complete or near absence. It means that the world as it is today cannot fully satisfy the desires of each and every one of its inhabitants because the resources at hand are limited—whether they are metals, food, or oil.

Therefore, all resources can assume the state of lack. One of the roles of the economy is to send those resources to places and markets where they are the most efficient and in highest demand. In other words, they must be allocated and distributed efficiently.

For example, milk can be sold as milk or used to produce yogurt or ice cream. The economic question here is, "Which of the possible products will yield the greatest benefit?" This "benefit function," coupled with the property of potential lack, creates conflict and competition that breach the harmony among people and remove them from a connection of reciprocity, care, and collaboration. This undermines the mutuality incumbent upon us in the global and connected world in which we live.

The economy expresses the relationships among us, yet it also affects them, as is evident from the lack and the egoistic profit function that create rivalry, coalitions, tensions, and conflicts. Because we are in a global economic crisis that stems from our incongruity with the connected world to which humanity has evolved, it is time to adapt our relations to interdependence to enable us to build a new economy. The variable, dependent upon the new goal function, is "maximizing" the well-being of the human society and achieving the optimal standard of living for all.

No Lack of Energy in the New, Balanced Economy

Industrialization, urbanization, and our modern consumer-oriented society turned consumption into a culture and a way of life. Teamed with the growth of population that crossed the seven billion threshold, humanity has been brought to the edge of a deadlock. This deadlock manifests in depletion of essential natural resources such as clean drinking water and oil.

American geophysicist, Marion King Hubbert, established in 1956 the Peak Oil Theory. The theory explains changes in the availability of oil and other fossil fuels in light of over-pumping and the resulting depletion of the resource. According to the theory, since oil is not a renewable resource, it is likely to assume that at some point in time the global oil production will peak and then gradually decline. Hubbert predicted the peak of oil production in the U.S., which occurred in 1971.

Hubbert's theory is under constant debate among academics due to the vast economic and social ramifications of oil depletion, since growth depends on the abundance of cheap and accessible energy. When the availability of that energy source declines, global growth will be affected. That assertion applies to individuals, as well as to firms. The passing of the peak of global production will manifest in a global scarcity of fuel fundamentally different from the shortages that came before it. This time, its basis will be geological rather than political, whereas previous crises occurred due to deliberate inefficiency of the oil extraction process.[104]

Currently, developed countries are trading CO2 emission quotas. Put differently, countries are trading their "right" to pollute the air. Air pollution is costing taxpayers heavily, and the trade of air pollution quotas is more proof that the economic system has gone out of control. Instead of thinking in terms of humane, harmonious existence among people and between humanity and Nature, where we strive to prevent or correct the damages we have caused the planet that sustains us, each country is striving to maximize its own benefits and narrow interests.

For example, the Kyoto Protocol strove to establish collaborations and set international standards to prevent the continued deterioration of the state of the Earth. Instead, the protocol has become a tool in the hands of industrialized powers to cover up their ambitions. They began to trade pollution quotas in order to continue the production race. The ecological solution seems to contradict the economic solution, and economic interests and short-range vision continue to prevail, despite the harm to the public good and the future of humanity.

Adapting the connection between people to what is required from the interdependence among us in the global and connected world will result in striving for congruence and harmony with Nature, demonstrating to us that balance is the optimal way of life.

The human tendency to focus on accumulating fortunes, over-consumption, and competition is depleting the non-renewable resources of Earth. Our inconsideration of our planet is in contrast with the interdependence that the global-integral world requires of us. If I pollute my habitat, the rest of us will

---

104   Kenneth S. Deffeyes, "Hubbert's Peak: The Impending World Oil Shortage," *Princeton University Press* (2002), http://www.trincoll.edu/~silverma/reviews_commentary/hubberts_peak.html

suffer the consequences. Pollution and inconsideration are destroying our entire society.

By over-producing, we prevent the regeneration of resources. If we shift to balanced consumption, based on relations that are in sync with the necessary relations in a global and interconnected world, we will not only stop damaging ecology, and indirectly the human society, but we will also allow Earth to recover and regenerate its resources.

The regeneration of forests, the arrest of extinction of plant and animal species, and the recovery of the fish population in the oceans are only some examples of the benefits we will derive. Since the energy crisis is hurting the resources available to us, solving it by changing people's approach will diminish the lack of natural resources. This will occur because demand will diminish due to the transition to a balanced economy, and because supply will grow due to Earth's natural regeneration processes. The result will be a welcome addition of resources for our use and our well-being.

WHAT WILL WE GAIN FROM THE CONSTANT INCREASE OF UNEMPLOYMENT, AND HOW?

The new, balanced economy—a result of mutual guarantee among people, between them and the state, and among all the countries—will expose great surpluses and reserves, reduce inefficiency in the job market, and prevent the kinds of financial damage caused by the current system. Moreover, the anticipated dramatic increase in the number of unemployed in the world will accelerate and support the process of matching interrelations among people to the global and interconnected world.

The transition away from over-consumption and competitive, aggressive, and bloated industry, which produces far beyond what humanity requires, means that industries and services will shrink. The current race requires so much effort, funding, and attention from the entire chain of production and consumption that returning to a sane economy will be greeted with a sigh of relief.

For the cost of average wages, which the state will save through unemployment, it will be possible to finance scholarships for those ejected from the job market, as well as fund the emergency education framework to be established for recipients of the scholarships. The purpose of the emergency education system will be to equip the unemployed with practical knowledge in personal finance and life skills, and will assist their integration into a changing world that will be based on mutual guarantee.

The contraction of production during the return to functional economy will not harm the ability of the marketplace to provide for all the needs of its citizens' sustenance. In a balanced economy, there is no need for 90% employment, nor even 50%! If only 20% of the work force were employed in agriculture, industry, and required services, it would suffice to satisfy the needs of the entire human society. Naturally, rotation among the workers and the unemployed can be applied, depending on the agreements that will be made in a society that follows the laws of mutual guarantee.

Thus, the change at hand is not a passing phase. Rather, it is a structural change in the global economy. In mutual guarantee, the symbiosis among people is complete, and those who choose to keep on working will be appreciated for their contribution to the collective well-being, and for the fact that their work enables humanity to keep evolving, existing in harmony among people, and between humanity and Nature.

The need to employ vast populations has created a colossal amount of redundant jobs, hidden unemployment, and bloating of mechanisms and bureaucracy, especially in the over-inflated public sector. A good example of such a faulty process is Greece, where the public sector is overblown and the country is on the verge of insolvency. One of the key requirements of the International Monetary Fund (IMF) of Greece is to substantially trim the size of its public sector. But Greece is only an example, albeit a rather extreme one, of a similar process that is occurring the world over.

In our current state of hidden unemployment and inefficiency, high wages inflate the expenses of the public sector, hindering the state's ability to service its citizens. From a purely economic perspective, a person who is occupied in a job that is not beneficial to society brings more good when he is *not* working, even when he receives unemployment benefits.

The anticipated growth in unemployment will not harm the economy or those who have lost their jobs if the emergency plan is activated and people are paid a sustenance scholarship, provided they join the educational and social framework that provides them with basic life skills. In today's complicated reality, they will learn how to adapt to the changes incumbent upon us by the global-integral world and become integrated in a society that lives by the principle of mutual guarantee. The expenditures saved, compared to the annual employment of such a worker, will be substantial enough to allow payment of sustenance scholarships to that person and to one additional person to provide for their basic needs. At the same time, it will teach them life skills and knowledge regarding the global and connected world, and the mutual guarantee.

For example, the average annual pay in England is £28,000 sterling (approximately $44,000 U.S.). Yet, an unemployed person aged 25 or more receives only £3,370 (approx $5,300) in unemployment benefits, adjusted to annual income. Even considering that the gap is lower in more welfare-oriented countries, the calculation is quite clear. If unemployment benefits are raised to approximately £13,000 ($20,000, roughly the average income of today's bottom fifth in the UK), and considering the above-described price reductions that will take place in the mutual guarantee economy, the state will be able to pay scholarships to two people to join the educational framework and adapt their personal finances to life in the new world.

It is important to note that the government's contribution to the Gross Domestic Product (GDP) is its added value, meaning the sum of payments that the government pays (or income that stems from the government).

Global unemployment will increase. It cannot be resolved with the traditional economic tools. President Obama's The American Jobs Act,[105] which focused on the U.S. job market and cost 450 billion dollars in tax incentives, was intended to boost the stalled American job market. Now, this Act joins three previous stimulus programs of different kinds that began in 2008. And as the previous programs failed, this plan is likely to fail, as well, as it was generated from the same old toolbox. The interdependence in the globally interconnected world appearing before us in this crisis necessitates different relations among us, and hence a new approach to solutions of economic problems.

Because all the industries in the connected world we live in depend on one another, unemployment will grow exponentially. The decline in income will necessarily induce a decline in consumption, and a natural transition will occur whereby industries will become proportionate to the needs of the people.

Unemployment is a natural result of the transition into proportionate consumption and the restoration of the "sanity" of the industry. That process will halt the exploitation of earth's depleting resources and in time will increase the resources available for humanity's use. The current inflated economic system is wasteful and causes social and environmental harm, demanding huge budgets to mend the damage. This is a vicious

---

105   http://www.whitehouse.gov/the-press-office/2011/09/08/fact-sheet-american-jobs-act

cycle whose toll on humanity is immense. The transition to a balanced economy will save the majority of those funds, which can then be turned toward the benefit of the public.

The financial sector, too, is blown out of proportion and is the main reason for the outbreak of the 2008 global crisis, from which the current crisis is a natural evolution. The pursuit of quick profits has become completely unrestrained, causing the financial and banking industries to inflate through reckless leveraging. By doing so, the mortgage banks and investment firms have created a sub-prime bubble, which exploded with a bang, igniting the global financial crisis. The damages from speculation and the resulting financial bubbles throughout the world amount to trillions of dollars. The effect of the loss of those trillions was felt by each of us, even if we were not aware that we were being affected.

The interdependence and the tight connections between the finance industry and the real economy caused the crisis in stock markets to spur a global recession. To succeed in the global and connected world we must sign an economic treaty and a social treaty, a mutual guarantee that will not allow such crises to occur because it will be clear to all that there we are interdependent. If we hurt others, we will be hurting ourselves.

AN ECONOMIC OPPORTUNITY

It is impossible to stop the natural process unfolding in the global economy. Rising unemployment, accompanied by a decline in consumption, will continue until it is stabilized on a reasonable level. Many countries—particularly the United States, where 70% of the GDP comes from private consumption—are faced with a deadlock because they lack the tools to cope with the new situation.

As unemployment spreads, consumption will decrease, the GDP will decline, the economy will slide into recession, and unemployment will rise even higher. However, we should not view this process as a crisis. Rather, it is an opportunity to change the paradigms that are based on individualism, competition, and self-centered benefits, which have brought us to our current plight. We have an opportunity to create a new and balanced economy that will bring all of us a far higher standard of living than we currently have.

The main goal of the new economic system, the balanced economy, should be the provision of a reasonable and fair standard of living to all citizens. Financing will not come from rash bloating of budgets, which can jeopardize the stability of the system, but from the surplus that will be revealed in society through the transitions discussed above. This will occur without the need to use the old economic, fiscal, and monetary tools that have proven themselves inadequate to deal with the current crisis.

Instead, to deal with the crisis we must begin by understanding its root. We must provide an expansive process of explanation, education, and construction of a society founded on values of mutual guarantee and solidarity. We must come to feel that the world is a single family. Through education and the influence of the environment on us, the current function will change into a function whose aim is to provide the reasonable needs to sustain individuals, families, and firms. Anything beyond this will be used for public benefit.

The process of mutual guarantee assures reciprocity. In a society that functions in mutual guarantee, every person knows that if he or she is lacking, that lack will be met. Such a person will not need to care for himself and will be free to create and produce for the benefit of all.

People will be appreciated by society according to their contributions to it, rather than by their personal fortunes or positions. This shift of mindset will cause great surpluses to appear, which were hidden in times when people cared only for their own benefit, assuming that no one would care for them should they need assistance. In a mutual guarantee-based economy, there is no need to save for a rainy day. As part of the socioeconomic treaty, it will be society's role to care for all of the people through agreed-upon taxation.

MUTUAL GUARANTEE—A PRICELESS ASSET

In addition to the advantages of reducing energy expenditures and transforming the job market, there are several benefits and surpluses that will arise in a mutual guarantee economy.

Housing: With rising foreclosures, falling prices, and risky mortgages, housing has been a problem in several countries, particularly in the U.S.. While millions have been evicted, millions of homes stand empty with no buyers in sight. In a society that follows the principle of mutual guarantee, people and banks will lend houses at the cost of overheads out of concern for others, and because such an act will reward them with great social acclaim. In a mutual guarantee society, those who own land and do not need it to live on will use that land to increase the supply for housing and provision of affordable accommodation.

Over-consumption: People consume far more than they need to sustain a reasonable standard of living. If we consider the products that we have and are not using, or that we replace simply because a newer model has been launched, we will see that by redistributing them, we can provide for the needs of the entire population without producing even a single new product. In other words, in most products there is no real lack, but rather unequal distribution due to our competitiveness and self-centered approach. When we establish reciprocal connections of mutual guarantee, we will discover that there is no lack of any product, but rather abundance and surplus.

Food prices and cost-of-living: According to a report by the Food and Agriculture Organization of the United Nations (FAO), "Roughly one third of the food produced in the world for human consumption every year—approximately 1.3 billion tons—gets lost or wasted."[106] These horrific data, combined with the knowledge that nearly 1 billion people worldwide are undernourished,[107] form an irreconcilable social paradox. Any reasonable person will see that establishing a system to preserve and properly distribute surplus food will solve the problem of hunger—and its subsequent illnesses—without any reform whatsoever.

Another paradox is food prices. Many countries are affected by high inflation, which primarily hurts those with lower incomes. In a society that follows the principle of mutual guarantee, such a problem would be resolved immediately. When we realize that humanity is indeed a single family, we will not want to throw away any food knowing that there are members of our family going to bed hungry each night.

The business sector: The education process that will adjust the current systems to one of interdependence will cause the business sector to adopt a different profit function. Instead of striving to maximize profit at the expense of the consumer and to minimize production costs at the expense of the employees, the new paradigm will strive to cover all production costs, and to direct profits toward public benefit. Firms will not be evaluated by the performance of their shares but by their contribution to society.

---

106   "Cutting food waste to feed the world: Over a billion tonnes squandered each year," *Food and Agriculture Organization of the United Nations* (May 11, 2011), http://www.fao.org/news/story/en/item/74192/icode/
107   "Global hunger declining, but still unacceptably high," *Food and Agriculture Organization of the United Nations*, Economic and Social Development Department (September 2010), www.fao.org/docrep/012/al390e/al390e00.pdf

This process will lower the price of food and basic products and will allow people to enjoy a reasonable standard of living. The rise in the cost of living in the last 20 years has increased social inequality and has driven hundreds of millions to the verge of poverty or beyond.[108]

Equitable division of income without government intervention: There is already evidence that beyond a reasonable level of income, happiness does not increase along with the increase in income.[109] Educating people about social solidarity, mutual guarantee, and conditioning appreciation of the social environment on prosocial activities will create among those earning in excess of what is needed for their sustenance a desire to contribute a portion of their income to the public. This will enable those with lower incomes to enjoy a sustainable standard of living. The satisfaction they will derive from the gratitude of society will increase the level of happiness among the givers far more than the fleeting satisfaction of purchasing another gadget, later to be thrown away as useless when the next generation of gadgets arrives a few months later.

A change of heart among tycoons and solving the issue of centralization of power: 1% of the world population controls 40% of global wealth.[110] Such a situation presents complicated economic and social issues, fostering resentment and a sense of injustice in the general population. The change of heart among

---

108   "Poverty Reduction and Equity," *The World Bank*, http://web.worldbank.org/WBSITE/ EXTERNAL/TOPICS/EXTPOVERTY/0,,contentMDK:23003429~pagePK:148956~piPK:21 6618~theSitePK:336992,00.html
109   Kahneman, D.; Krueger, A.; Schkade, D.; Schwarz, N.; Stone, A. (2006). "Would you be happier if you were richer? A focusing illusion". *Science* 312 (5782): 1908-10
110   James Randerson, "World's richest 1% own 40% of all wealth, UN report discovers," *The Guardian* (December 6, 2006), http://www.guardian.co.uk/money/2006/dec/06/business. internationalnews,
Joseph Stiglitz (abridged/edited by Henry Makow), "1% Controls 40% of US Wealth," *henrymakow.com* (April 10, 2011), http://www.henrymakow.com/stiglitz.html,
Rachel Ehrenberg, "Financial world dominated by a few deep pockets," *Science News* (September 24, 2011), http://www.sciencenews.org/view/generic/id/333389/title/Financial_ world_dominated_by_a_few_deep_pockets

the few who control such a large portion of the world's wealth—
as society learns to live by the principles of mutual guarantee—
will bring them to relinquish most of their wealth in return for
social acclaim and lasting financial stability. At the same time,
the released funds will secure the well-being of the remaining
99%, defusing the social time bomb of economic inequality and
strengthening social cohesion.

Instead of controlling the world's fortunes, the world's
super-rich will enjoy wall-to-wall appreciation from the public.
Naturally, they will retain sufficient funds to provide for their
own well-being, but beyond that they will be valued for their
contribution to the public and to the environment, rather than
for the number of private jets that they own. If they are educated
in the value of mutual guarantee, they will donate those funds
voluntarily.

Surpluses in state budgets: Currently, government offices
struggle against each other, resembling our own behavior
against our fellow citizens. Every office, acting as a separate
entity, fights to boost its own budget. Studies in public
policy, particularly the "Public Choice" theory, argue that
a bureaucrat strives to increase his or her office's budget to
gain prestige, money, and status.[111] The result, however, is
inefficient distribution of funds. When all government offices
feel like parts of a single family, many surpluses in the budget
will surface and the public sector will be managed much more
efficiently, to the benefit of the public.

A secure future: As explained above, the new norms and
values implanted in society will change the perception of profit
from maximum personal gain to maximum social benefit. This
shift will expose great surpluses that are already available but

---

111   Niskanen, W. A. (1987). "Bureaucracy" In Charles K. Rowley, ed. *Democracy and Public Choice*. Oxford: Basil Blackwell

are hidden. We will be able to provide a reasonable standard of living to every single family.

When considering the immense influence of the environment on a person, we understand that the change described above is both realistic and necessary. The norms and behaviors designed by society will alter our economic conduct and adjust it to the global-integral system. We naturally strive to agree with our social environment, to receive its appreciation. For this reason, a change in the perception of society will change the conduct of individuals and societies, and will allow us to adapt our economic and social systems to a new reality—one that is good for all.

ECONOMISTS AND EXPERTS IN THE NEW WORLD

ECONOMISTS WILL PLAY A KEY ROLE IN ADAPTING THE HUMAN SOCIETY TO THE GLOBAL-INTEGRAL WORLD

Key Points
- The network of self-centered ties woven in the world since the industrial revolution has exhausted its potential and led humanity into a global economic crisis.
- The most prominent economists are bewildered. All attempts to resolve the economic crisis using the traditional toolbox have failed because the existing paradigms no longer match the global-integral reality.
- Without a much needed transformation of the economic paradigms to match the laws of the global-integral world, humanity will not overcome the problems threatening its existence.

- Learning the laws of the global-integral world is a precondition for understanding the network of connections and for building a new society.
- Economists and experts in social science have a key role to play in adapting the economic ties among all parts of the human society in the global-integral world.

"The ideas of economists and political philosophers, both when they are right and when they are wrong, are more powerful than is commonly understood. Indeed the world is ruled by little else. ...I am sure that the power of vested interests is vastly exaggerated compared with the gradual encroachment of ideas. ...But, soon or late, it is ideas, not vested interests, which are dangerous for good or evil."[112]

~J.M. Keynes

THE UNIQUE ROLE OF ECONOMISTS

The economic crisis is arousing anxiety among economists and decision-makers throughout the world. The global crisis is the world's worst economic crisis since the 1930s' Great Depression. It touches each of us and compels us to not only carefully examine the causes of the crisis, but to actively address the deformations that have grown in our imbalanced economy and correct them. The unique role of economists is to help the rest of us to understand the crisis and to lead the mending of the global economic system.

THE CRISIS OF ECONOMIC THOUGHT

When analyzing the causes of the crisis, it appears that the existing economic paradigms no longer suit the global reality of our lives. While the old thought patterns that have dominated the world for more than a hundred years seem significantly

---

112   John Maynard Keynes, *The General Theory of Employment, Interest and Money*, (U.K., Palgrave Macmillan, 1936), pp 383-4

lacking, new thought patterns that match the current reality and would help cope with the crisis are simply nonexistent.

Many economists and financiers disagree on modes of action or predictions, but that only emphasizes the faults of the existing paradigms in addressing the world's economic and financial challenges. Nevertheless, the crisis waits for no one. Each day, as it expands and becomes more systemic, the danger of global economic shutdown intensifies.

At the end of the day, it is a crisis that stems from the gap between the currently prevailing economic thought, and the concept that should prevail in the global-integral world we live in. As Prof. Joseph Stiglitz put it in a lecture titled, "Imagining an Economics that Works: Crisis, Contagion and the Need for a New Paradigm," "The test of any science is prediction. And if you can't predict something as important as a global financial crisis or the magnitude of the one that we are going through, obviously something's wrong with your model."[113]

A NEW TOOLBOX IN ECONOMIC RESEARCH

In studying living organisms, the scientist first simplifies and explains how the various organs function, then explains about the different systems and their interrelations, thus performing analysis and synthesis. Studying the interrelations among systems, scientists from life sciences point to a unifying force that sustains all the cells in an organism. The cells absorb the beneficial and secrete what is not beneficial, thus creating a life of balance and harmony.

As a physiologist must be equipped with the right tools for that field of research, an economist needs the right tools for his or her studies. An absence of appropriate tools to build or define

---

113   "Short films from the 2011 Lindau Nobel Laureate Meeting in Economic Sciences," *The New Palgrave Dictionary of Economics Online*, http://www.dictionaryofeconomics. com/resources/news_lindau_meeting http://www.dictionaryofeconomics.com/resources/ news_lindau_meeting (see Stiglitz's lecture, minute 1:36)

a new model impedes the finding of solutions to the current global crisis. The new model addresses the fact that today the system is global and connected by ties of mutual dependence. For now, that model may not be entirely clear to us, due to limitations imposed by the economic theory that has evolved over the previous century.

NUMEROUS INTERCONNECTIONS THAT CANNOT BE RELIABLY PREDICTED

The purpose of every theory is to simplify reality, and theories in economics are no exception. However, every researcher knows that perfect congruence between theory and practice is seldom found. The current economic theory assumes that each person wishes to maximize his or her personal benefit, and describes a system of relations between consumers, manufacturers, firms, and countries according to that premise.

The theory propounds that each element in the system has a different set of priorities and seeks to achieve the best results for itself. These elements join into more complex systems, such as firms, corporations, markets, and countries that function in a global and integral world. This last element, the global, integral world, is what poses the difficulties in building economic models that consider *all* the stages of decision making in the chain. This is one reason why the current economic theory is imperfect and limited in its applicability.

INABILITY TO QUANTIFY AND PREDICT HUMAN BEHAVIOR

Economics uses statistical tools that allow for isolation of variables to detect which connections repeat themselves, and under what conditions. Using these statistical tools, researchers learn from past events and build models of behavior over time. They can use these mathematical tools because it is possible to quantify the various parameters. However, what happens when the models need to include unquantifiable parameters? Human behavior is just such a parameter, and because economics relates directly to human behavior, it renders the entire field of study limited and inexact.

The reason why human behavior is unpredictable is that making decisions includes elements that are not always rational. Only by combining different methods of research, different paradigms—such as classical economics, which relates to quantifiable elements, and behavioral economics, which relates to human nature—is it possible to study the entire system. This allows researchers to understand human behavior, recognize the boundaries of the system, and understand the connections that bring it into balance. Only when we achieve all that can we accurately detect the causes of the imbalance that has led to the current crisis.

The integrative approach is a precondition, valid particularly today when a whole new economic system that is radically different from its predecessor is being built. The new system is founded on the laws of integration of the entire system. As in the study of organisms as closed systems, in the new economic system an economist will be able to follow changes, define causalities, and quantify parameters for the proper functioning of the interrelations among the elements in the system.

THE NEW ECONOMIC THEORY—GLOBAL INTEGRATION

Thus far, the economic theory has managed to characterize the behavior of economic units on the level of particular units, as well as on the general level. However, the theory worked only as long as units could be looked at as particular elements. This created a natural division into segments of economic research, such as "labor economics," which seeks to understand the dynamics of the labor market, or "macroeconomics," which deals with the performance, structure, behavior, and decision-making of the economy as a whole. That division sufficiently explained the connections among the economic units and the dependence among them within the market of each specific country, including cases of closed markets or trade relations among different countries.

However, economics did not succeed in integrating these study units into a single, solid piece that ties all the units into one, as required in the global and connected world. The inability to connect the systems into one is the primary challenge of economics today. The disconnect makes them incongruent with the laws of integration that are manifesting in today's interconnected world.

Today, the economic and financial units operate in a single global environment. They are tied to each other by necessity and depend on each other in ever-tightening connections. It is an evolutionary process that has now reached a critical point because the tools in the hands of economists are no longer effective. They were developed and perfected in a world entirely different from that of today.

Previously, one could explain how connections among economic and financial units were formed. It was possible to express the connection among distinct elements in a quantifiable manner. Now an integrative law operates throughout the world, taking into account *all* the possible connections. Matching the current economic and social systems to that law will necessarily lead to a world that aspires to balance and harmony precisely because it regards all the possible connections. Conversely, incongruity with that law will be experienced as an escalating crisis.

THE FALL OF THE OLD PARADIGMS THAT LED TO THE CRISIS

The current economic paradigm that led us into this crisis created—among other ills—a legal and moral foundation to exploit cheap labor, primarily in East Asia, and to over-consume our natural resources. That foundation has led to mutual dependence from which we can no longer escape. The U.S., for instance, has become a superpower of financial services and consumption. China, on the other hand, as well as India and other developing nations, have become the world's factories. The global system is more connected than ever, and economists must build an economic paradigm that supports that mutual dependence.

Humanity has evolved from individualism, competitiveness, and manipulations into an interconnected global system that requires economists to devise a new paradigm that reflects it. This paradigm must take into consideration the fact that we are living in a global-integral system, and only when we understand its laws will we be able to properly establish the economic connections that will lead us to a life of happiness and balance.

Globalization is no longer a great discovery. It is a reality to which economists often refer in their statements and speeches. Economist Mark Vitner described the global interconnectedness in a rather palpable manner: "It's like trying to unscramble scrambled eggs. It just can't be done that easily. I don't know if it can be done at all."[114]

And yet, the solutions economists offer decision-makers still rely on tools from the obsolete paradigm of the world of separate entities. They suggest such steps as cutting interest rates, pouring funds into the system (euphemism for printing money), or reducing government expenses.

114 Associated Press, "Recession will likely be longest in postwar era," *MSNBC* (March, 2009), http://www.msnbc.msn.com/id/29582828/wid/1/page/2/

Perhaps such monetary and fiscal means could provide first aid, but they are completely ineffective when it comes to treating the roots of the crisis and securing a viable, solid, and sustainable economic system. These solutions fail because they miss the root of the crisis—the mismatch between the functioning of the current economic system and the required functioning within the global-integral system. The bailout programs of the 2008 financial crisis relied on the old theories and hence failed bitterly, leaving us to face an even more threatening version of that crisis just three years later.

By trying to address the new problems without understanding the laws by which the global-integral system operates, we are only aggravating the crisis. Moreover, the incongruity of economic systems with the current modus operandi of the world puts them in immediate danger of economic collapse, revolutions, and civil wars. The Arab Spring of 2011, now spilling into 2012, is an example of the dangers that economic pressures can pose. The clout of extremist and nationalistic elements and parties throughout the world is rising. The protests in Europe and the U.S. can lead to violence, undermine domestic peace, rattle the political systems within countries, and even increase the chance of a full-blown war.

Economists have the duty and the responsibility to acquire a thorough understanding of the laws of the new world economy. In it, laws reflect systems of human relations that are moving toward collaboration, synergy, solidarity, cohesion, and harmony. Only when economists grasp that new direction will they be able to develop proper models to describe the global-integral system and how it should work. This, in turn, will lead to establishing an entirely new economy.

MISPERCEPTION

To demonstrate the connection between the laws of the global-integral system and our ability to identify its characteristics we must turn to other fields of science. First, we need to realize that we do not perceive reality for what it is, but for what we *believe* it to be. In an online essay titled, "Objective Science: an Inherent Oxymoron," Dr. Johnston Laurance, former director at the National Institute of Child Health and Human Development, wrote, "All scientific observation—even at the most fundamental level—is affected by the observer's consciousness. In this regard, the statement, 'I'll see it when I believe it' is more apropos than its commonly stated converse."[115]

In that essay, Dr. Laurance quoted several other like-minded scientists and thinkers, such as 19th century neurologist Jean Martin Charcot, considered the founder of modern neurology: "In the last analysis, we see only what we are ready to see, what we have been taught to see. We eliminate and ignore everything that is not part of our prejudices."

Thus, to devise the right solution to the crisis, we must first adjust ourselves to it so that the tools with which we approach the problems will be the right tools. Are there economists who can already offer viable solutions to the crisis? Regrettably, for many years academia has taught us how to produce financial wealth, rather than economic balance and harmony in our society. In order to even approach the crisis in the right frame of mind, we must become re-educated about many aspects of the economy.

STUDYING THE GLOBAL-INTEGRAL REALITY

The vast gap between the global-integral reality to which the human society has evolved, and the current economic paradigms, which have not significantly changed since the industrial

---

115   Laurance Johnston, "Objective Science: An Inherent Oxymoron" (April 2007), http://brentenergywork.com/OBJECTIVE_SCIENCE_ARTICLE.htm

revolution, is the real reason for the crisis. Understanding the gap is the first step toward solving the crisis, and this is the great challenge that economists face today.

Integral thinking, which takes into account all the possible connections among the parts of the system, can provide a researcher with tools to perform accurate calculations and predictions of any kind.. It can tell economists what they need to change in the existing systems and how. But first they must rid themselves of the old thought-patterns and study the thought-patterns of the global-integral system, and the incumbent economic paradigm. The first to adopt the integral thought-pattern must be those whose role makes them the most sensitive to changes and dynamics in the human society, such as economists, politicians, and sociologists.

AN OPPORTUNITY TO BUILD A NEW ECONOMY

The existing systems cannot be discarded offhandedly. We have a major challenge ahead of us that entails a profound change of perception on our part. Such a change requires transforming our thinking from models of personal and local benefit to models that focus first and foremost on meeting the necessities of all people, replacing the pursuit of wealth, over-consumption, and status symbols with new, nonmaterial benefits that come from contributing to the global-integral human society.

The opportunity before economists is a rare gem, a once in many generations event. Humanity is at the threshold of a new era in which new causalities appear. Economists have the privilege of being the pioneers who will adjust the structure of the human society to the new reality. Those among them who are wise enough to build the new economy in line with the principle that we are all connected in a global-integral network will be well rewarded. The fate of the world rests on their ability to make that change and lead humanity to global prosperity and abundance.

ECONOMIC MESSAGE BOX

1) A global-integral world:

- **Global:** "Globalization" refers to the increasingly international relationships involving culture, people, and economic activity. Most often it refers to economics: the planetary distribution of locations where goods and services are produced, enabled through the reduction of barriers to international trade such as tariffs, export fees, and import quotas. Globalization has accompanied and contributed to economic growth in developed and developing countries through increased specialization and the principle of comparative advantage (the ability of a person or a country to produce a particular good or service at a lower cost). The term can also refer to the transnational circulation of ideas, languages, and popular culture.

- **Integral:** entire, complete, whole. Also, consisting or composed of parts that together constitute a whole.

Those two processes, globalization and integration, are interlinked and describe the new global-integral world. The development of technology, the internet, cellular communication, world trade, and the financial markets have accelerated the evolution of humanity toward a new and connected world.

The wheel cannot be turned back; it is impossible to resist the process of global integration. The recent crises have made humanity realize that our lives will never be as they were before. The acceleration of globalization and the transformation of the world into a global village, where interdependence and mutual influence on one another are increasing, compel us not only to be considerate of each other, but to actually empathize with and fully partake in each other's lives.

The global crisis originated in our current connections, based on individualism, competition, and egoism, compared to the kind of connections that are now required in a state of interdependence in a global-integral world. The solution to the global crisis begins with establishing new kinds of connections among us, which will better suit the world we now live in.

Because the crisis is a systemic problem, if people connect in mutual guarantee and solidarity, and work in reciprocity toward a single goal—to be in balance with the global-integral world—we will create an enlightened world. That world will sustain all of us with abundance and ease while we maintain harmony among ourselves and between us and Nature.

In economy and finance, our mutual dependence is especially obvious. It is indisputable. Stock markets around the world have a tight correlation that only increases in times of crisis. The bonds market is a global mechanism by which countries raise tremendous amounts of money from one another, in effect financing each other's economies. The economy itself reflects tight cross-border relations, and many firms have become global corporations that manufacture in many countries and sell their products throughout the world. Today, no country is self-sufficient, and the global economic crisis proves it every day.

2) **Mutual guarantee:** The global-integral world demands a transformation in the way we perceive human relations. These relations must be based on care for others and mutual concern, just like a family. First and foremost, this change entails a personal shift in the way we connect with others. This will then be translated into a social and economic treaty, dealing with every issue and need on the individual, community, state, and international levels. The mutual guarantee economy will rely on a transition from individualism, competitiveness, and self-centered profit function that aims to maximize personal gain, even at others' expense, into a balanced economy that provides for the basic needs of every person. The aim of that economy will be toward public well-being and closing socioeconomic gaps by consent of all parties and with complete transparency.

3) **The round table:** In order to tend to the basic needs of all the people, we must come together in round-table discussions where all are equal, just like in a family. Politicians, economists, sociologists, and experts from many disciplines will put their heads together and ponder the best way to serve our extended family. This is the only way to formulate the right order of priorities, through broad consensus that is then implemented within national budgets and international relations. The transparency of the round-table discussions will maintain the legitimacy of the mechanism and support the public confidence that decisions are taken with public well-being in mind.

4) **Information and Education:** The key to personal change and to adapting our relations to increased mutual dependence and stronger interconnections is education and provision of information. This is the only way we will advance toward mutual guarantee.

The curricula will include, among other topics:

- Personal finance.
- Life skills, aimed at assisting people in functioning in one's immediate economic and financial environment, and coping with the ramifications of the crisis on people's personal lives.
- Informing people regarding the different aspects of life in a global-integral world, understanding the nature of reality in such a world, its causes, the connections between globalization and the required changes in one's connections with others, and stressing the influence of the social environment on a person. The transition to a life of solidarity and mutual guarantee is impossible without the social environment's support and encouragement of that process.
- Mutual guarantee as a way of life—inculcating the social skills necessary for a sustainable and calm life in a global and connected world.

THE GLOBAL ECONOMIC CRISIS

1) **The economy expresses the nature of human relations:** The economy is an expression of human nature and reflects our human relations. This is why it must match the level of development of humanity. Thus, we must understand the characteristics of the global-integral reality, where we are all interdependent. The integral reality emphasizes the need to achieve mutual guarantee in order to obtain

economic and social prosperity and utilize the advantages of adjusting human relations to the global-integral system. The laws of the new, mutual guarantee economy will reflect this transformation in human relations. Only such a process will guarantee that the economy is stable, efficient, and maintains a sustainable balance.

2) **The reason for the economic crisis is the gap between the existing system and the one required in a global-integral world:** The crisis is first and foremost a crisis of human relations, resulting from the chasm between the individualistic and competitive nature of our current life-systems and the systems required in the global and connected world. That world dictates that we connect by creating ties of mutual guarantee, caring for each other's needs, and cooperating for everyone's benefit, including our own.

3) **The shattered economy is not the reason for the crisis, but its result:** Dealing with the global crisis must be thorough, addressing not only the symptoms, but changing the fundamental values of society and human relations. Only such a change will lead to the construction of a new economy, a just, more prosocial and balanced one. Only if we understand that the solution is in our relations with one another will we be able to find the right solutions for the crisis.

4) **The need for a new paradigm:** Neither the method nor the existing economic systems and theories were built or are intended to cope with a global-integral reality. Thus, the paradigms must be changed from the root. A new global economic theory is required, based on the premise that people conduct relations of mutual guarantee, and aspire to an altruistic socioeconomic model that demonstrates the advanced stages of a society that has adopted such relations as a way of life. If we remain in the current

capitalistic paradigm, based on the principle of "the invisible hand," we are hindering our ability to carry out the required change because economists and theoreticians support minimal government intervention in the market forces. They assume that the optimum balance will evolve naturally, for the benefit of the people whom those models are meant to serve.

5) **Replacing the economic toolbox:** The traditional economic toolbox for dealing with crises has failed us in this crisis. All the bailouts, rescue programs, and incentives given throughout the world relied on a single, old and familiar economic school by which the solution to the crisis lies in different combinations of monetary and fiscal expansions (depending on the country). All the bailout and rescue programs since 2008 not only failed, but aggravated the crisis by preventing us from treating its cause, although they did try to cope with the symptoms. We must urgently assume a new paradigm, as our current one is inadequate for the new network—the global socioeconomic system into which the world has evolved and the interdependence that this network has created.

6) **The crisis as an opportunity:** The economic and financial crisis is leading experts and decision-makers to realize that there is a need to adjust human relations and the socioeconomic systems derived from them to the required form of relations in a global-integral world. That world is pulling people closer together, prodding them to care for one another, and cooperate sincerely. It is leading them toward social cohesion, demanding that we replace aggressive and exaggerated competition with concord with the laws of the global-integral system. Narrowing the gaps between the systems will result in immediate relief in the crisis.

CHARACTERISTICS OF A BALANCED ECONOMY

1) **New profit and utility functions:** Reality dictates that we adjust the current economic and social systems to ones based on mutual consideration, collaboration, synergy, sharing information and resources, and balanced consumption. We must also unify economic, fiscal, and monetary mechanisms. These new systems express mutual guarantee, while the current economy is based on maximizing personal utility and profit, competitiveness, and stimulating inherent conflict among people and countries.

2) **Detaching income from consumption:** Every person will be able to purchase products and services according to need for a reasonable standard of living, regardless of income, provided everyone works and contributes to society according to their ability. In other words, everyone will do for society all they can, and will receive from society what they need for sustenance. Reciprocity and transparency will play key roles here. Detaching income from consumption will apply to everyone, but it does not mean that income, ownership of property and possessions, or contributing to the public benefit will be equal among everyone.

3) **Relative, idiosyncratic equality:** The mutual guarantee economy will bring with it drastic narrowing of socioeconomic inequality until it is completely annihilated. Society does not need to forcefully equalize everyone by arbitrarily distributing income, services, and material resources. Rather, distribution should be relative and individualistic—to each according to their particular needs for basic, reasonable living. A reasonable standard of living will be determined as "that which guarantees for every person the provision of life's necessities, and allows for comfortable living according to the specific needs of a person or a family." This standard will be in accord with the standard of living that is the norm in one's

immediate environment, meaning a standard of living above the poverty line for all. That standard will be determined by round table consensus (see this chapter, section "General," item 3). Equality will manifest in fairness of resource distribution, complete transparency of the decision-making process, full participation of the individual in the effort to provide for self and for family, and contributing to society's general well-being to the best of one's ability.

4) **Securing a reasonable standard of living:** A guaranteed standard of living will be secured for all, which suffices to maintain oneself on a reasonable level. Services and products will include housing, healthcare, education from birth to death, food, clothing, and anything that individuals and families need to live comfortably according to the economic abilities of the general society. This entails a standard of living that is above the poverty line, as described in the above item. As a result, some individuals or families will rise in their standard of living, and some will decline. However, the entire process will take place with everyone's consent and a sense of mutual responsibility and concern for each other, as is suitable for a society that has adopted mutual guarantee as a way of life. Informing, educating, and the influence of the environment are necessary elements in inculcating the required changes toward relative equality and securing a reasonable standard of living for all.

5) **A balanced economy:** Balanced consumption is imperative in this new, balanced economy. Adapting human interrelations to the dependence between them in the global-integral world will change the entire economic paradigm, not only consumption. It will move from a competitive, overblown, self-centered, and wasteful economy, into a balanced, stable, functional, and collaborative economy, and at more advanced stages, it will even become altruistic. All economic

systems–production, commerce, consumption, the financial system, and the social system will be adapted to the precise size required to provide humanity with all it needs for reasonable consumption, no less, and no more.

6) **Growth:** The pursuit of economic growth as society's prime goal does not serve the welfare of the public. It creates pressures and causes much economic and social harm. The transition to a balanced economy will render the system that venerates growth irrelevant. We will stop measuring a country's economic success by the percentage of growth of its GDP. The new economic goal of a country will be to provide all its citizens with what they need to sustain them. Beyond that, all national and personal resources will be aimed at developing and realizing the personal and collective potential of the citizens.

7) **Surpluses in the new economy:** A mutual guarantee-based economy will produce substantial surpluses in financial, economic, and natural resources. When we know that there is someone to take care of our needs under any circumstances, we will not need to keep reserves in property or money. Firms and countries will also follow that principle, and the surpluses will manifest in an abundance of natural resources, an increase of free land and rentable apartments, and freed resources due to the cessation of over-consumption of pre-prepared food and farmland products that are currently thrown away instead of being distributed. It will also manifest in increasing people's surpluses, along with the fair division of income, voluntary changes among tycoons, who will act to narrow inequality, and government offices that do not need to keep reserves for themselves. Due to the importance of this concept in the new economy, we dedicated the chapter, "Surplus and Improving the Public's Well-Being," entirely to that topic.

8) **Satisfaction from giving:** In a mutual guarantee-based economy, materialism will take its natural place—to provide for necessities. Satisfaction and the drive for work will come from the desire to be part of a society that lives by the principle of mutual guarantee among people, without additional income or possessions. Instead, gratification will come from providing for others' needs and from contributing to the general well-being. Our achievements will come from our contribution to the new socioeconomic treaty, from the desire to help others develop, and from the reciprocity of human relations.

   Satisfaction from giving is a result of a gradual inner change, through the influence of the environment, the provision of information, and education for mutual guarantee.

9) **An emergency plan for dealing with unemployment:** Unemployment will continue to rise due to the crisis and because of the necessary transition from an overblown, competitive economy into a balanced and functional one. Hundreds of millions of people will become unemployed and will thus require immediate attention. This socioeconomic time-bomb has the potential to destroy families, increase inequality, divide society, and could deteriorate into violence and social and governmental instabilities. The emergency plan for dealing with unemployment according to the principle of mutual guarantee, in the framework of the global-integral world, will include paying a fair sustenance-scholarship provided that one participates in an educational framework, to be established by the state. Participation will be regarded as working. For details on the content and advantages of the emergency plan for the state and for the people, see chapter, "Emergency Plan for Unemployment."

10) **Unifying government and financial mechanisms:** Currently, several international institutions, primarily in education, economy, and health—such as the World Bank, the International Monetary Fund, or UNESCO—reflect the international community's recognition of the need for mutual assistance, sharing of information, and cross-border and cross-culture collaboration. The new connection among people in the framework of the socioeconomic treaty called "mutual guarantee" will accelerate international collaboration.

    We are living within a single, closed economic system where one country cannot act only for its own interests, but rather with a sense of responsibility and connection to other countries. Therefore, it is only natural that international collaboration will increase and deepen, including unification of monetary and fiscal instruments in line with the laws of the global-integral world, recognizing that an integral system can have only one chief.

11) **The social tycoon:** In a mutual guarantee-based socioeconomic system, tycoons will have their rightful place. The required equality in a harmonious system is a relative and idiosyncratic one—according to one's needs and to the extent to which one fulfills one's potential contribution to society. Educating humanity toward mutual guarantee will change the values of tycoons from wanting to dominate and maximize their gain at the expense of consumers to extending to others new, prosocial values. The moguls will receive social approbation from society not because of their fancy cars, private jets, or their mansions, but because of their contribution to society, to the environment, to the country, and to the world. At the same time, tycoons will be able to continue using their unique skills so society can benefit from their abilities to produce wealth. This will

provide the tycoons with gratification, just as in a family, the main provider enjoys his or her ability to provide for the well-being of the entire family.

12) **The mutual guarantee index:** Today there are mechanisms for measuring economic and social inequality or the quality of life. When a mutual guarantee index is developed, we will be able to measure the degree to which firms, countries, and organizations implement the principle of mutual guarantee and the balanced economy described in this book. The index will also measure our progress toward mutual guarantee.

BENEFITS OF THE NEW ECONOMY

1) **Equal standard of living for all:** An economic policy based on mutual consideration will lead to allocating necessary public resources to raising lower income classes above the poverty line. At the same time, workshops and training in life skills and personal finance will help develop personal and economic independence. Living beyond one's means, over-consumption, and reckless use of credit have become a global pandemic that requires treatment. These have played a major role in the global economic crisis that has been going on since 2008, if not before.

2) **Reducing the cost of living:** When greed is no longer the basis of our commercial and economic relations, when each of us settles for a reasonable profit and does not strive to maximize profits at the expense of others, prices of products and services will plunge toward their real cost. The prime beneficiaries of the deflation will be the lower income classes. The reduction of the cost of living will reduce inequality and the social and economic gaps in society.

3) **Narrowing inequality and social gaps:** A phenomenon that has become more evident in the global economy is the constant increase in inequality. This is the main reason for

the worldwide social unrest. When we relate to one another like family, we will not be able to tolerate inequality among us or among countries in the international community. Instead of tension and fear of revolution or violence, the mutual guarantee economy will produce broad consent on the need to narrow the economic gaps, thus maintaining the stability of the system. Diminishing inequality means, among other things, economic and social concessions on the part of the upper classes, education and influence of the environment toward mutual guarantee, and an effective deliberation mechanism, known as "the round table." These will guarantee that decisions are made in transparency and fairness, reflecting the social and economic consensus required by the relationships of mutual guarantee among all people.

In return, those who can contribute to everyone's well-being will receive social acclaim and approbation. At the same time, those who receive assistance will enjoy a life of dignity and will appreciate the new system for having improved their economic and social status. Moreover, the mutual guarantee economy will guarantee that gaps existing today will not be duplicated in the future because the system will be balanced, stable, and based on high social cohesion.

4) **A genuine reform in the budget:** The only element that will enable us to create social justice in mutual guarantee, while noting the well-being of every individual in society—without breaching the budget—is the sense that we are all in the same boat and must cooperate for mutual benefit. We must determine a more equitable order of priorities in national budgets from broad consensus, instead of acting like wrestlers in the ring. There should be an economy managed with transparency, one that allows everyone to understand and influence how decisions are made.

5) **Improving human relations at work and the individual-firm-state relations:** In a mutual guarantee-based economy, economic and governmental systems will become friendly toward people under the umbrella of mutual guarantee—catering to citizens, rather than to governments. Similar improvements will take place in the authorities' treatment of firms and in relations between the business sector and the state's tax authorities.

6) **Trust:** The transition to another economy will be gradual. First, there will be dynamics of change and hope, a new spirit in society, a sense of cohesion and personal security. The anxiety and fear of being used and abused will give way to voluntary concessions and gestures in many areas, such as housing and rent prices, wage agreements that are fair to all sides, simpler and more efficient bureaucracy that truly serves the public, fair and honest banks, or garages that fix only what requires fixing and at a reasonable cost. All these examples have one thing in common—a sense of trust in others, a feeling that is so desperately needed in these insane times.

7) **An efficient decision-making process:** The new economy will be conducted with transparency. People will be able to see how decisions are made and will be able to influence them. The sense of transparency, along with involvement in the process, will create sympathy with the decisions made. Many studies in organizational behavior show that when we partake in a process, we tend to support decisions even when we are not in complete agreement with them. This is the way toward the feeling that we are so badly missing—the sense of fairness, our ability to approach decision-makers, and the need for social justice. This is the only way for the transformations in society and in the economy to be successful. There will be a progressive welfare policy, and inequality will

be narrowed down through public deliberation and broad consent. Collaboration, sharing, and transparent decision-making will contribute to the stability and sustainability of the socioeconomic system.

8) **Balanced consumption:** The over-consumption that has become such an important part of our lives will, with the encouragement of our social environment, gradually, and through broad consent, make way for balanced consumption. Private consumption will return to normalcy instead of the exaggerated consumption that relies on commercials and social pressure whose sole purpose is to persuade us to purchase products and services we do not need. Many redundant products and services will disappear, and consumption will rely on practical calculations of utility and service in our daily lives at a reasonable level that is the norm in our respective environments. Brands as social status will be replaced with contribution to society and participation in community life and work for the common good.

Following the decline in demand, the cost of living will drop and a reasonably dignified living standard will be accessible to all. That process has already begun and is connected to the crisis and the gradual transition of humanity from a competitive, wasteful economy that is self-centered and unequal, to a balanced and functional economy whose goal is to provide for the basic needs of every person.

9) **Improving the state of ecology and Nature:** The shift from exploitative economy and over consumption—which deplete natural resources and damage man and the Earth—into balanced consumption will reduce the amount of industrial production and the number of unnecessary products. These processes will contribute significantly to improving the planet's ecology: air and water pollution will decrease, the mountains of waste will be reduced dramatically, and

the plundering of energy and natural resources will cease. The return to normalcy of consumption and production, to equality and fairness in division of resources, will guarantee that the use of natural resources is done at a pace that allows earth to replenish its treasures.

There are plenty of resources on this Earth to provide for the entire human race and all the species on earth for a long, long time. The mutual guarantee economy is a balanced and harmonious economy, and hence will be friendly toward Planet Earth, on which our lives depend.

A profound advantage of the mutual guarantee is that in a balanced and harmonious system, the likelihood of conflicts among nations and countries, even aggressive diplomacy, is virtually nonexistent. Power struggles, protectionism, tariffs, currency struggles, and exploiting weaknesses of other countries will make way for the new economy—in the spirit of mutual guarantee.

Appendices

PREVIOUS PUBLICATIONS BY THE ARI INSTITUTE

WE, WE, WE

That we are in the midst of a "global crisis" is no longer in question. Since there is also ample evidence that the term "globalization" covers far more than the correlation between global financial markets, a more accurate meaning of the term should address the interconnected nature of society as a whole. We are "global" not just in the financial sense, but also, if not primarily, in the social, if not emotional sense. Our emotions affect those of other people so intensely that they can start social blazes in country after country, passing from one hot spot to the next via the wires that connect the World Wide Web.

The "Arab Spring" has expanded far beyond the Arab world. In each country, the causes and the manifestations of the protests wear a different "attire." In Egypt, mass demonstrations overthrew the government. In Syria, the people's heroic resistance in the face of carnage is a testimony to the profound spiritual change that has arisen. Citizens simply cannot tolerate tyranny any longer.

In Israel, demonstrations are peaceful but of an unprecedented magnitude. In the demonstration that took place on Saturday, August 6, 2011, 300,000 people participated, roughly one out of every 22 Israelis. If one out of 22 Americans were to participate in a demonstration, it would require space for roughly 14 million people.

In Spain, the tent camps of protestors have been standing for months, with neither a solution nor dispersion of the camp dwellers in sight. In the U.K., violent riots have erupted that seem to baffle Prime Minister David Cameron, who was caught off-guard vacationing in Italy. Even Chile is now on the protest map with violent student demonstrations. According to a CNN report,[116] in August of 2011, "More than 60,000 [students] demonstrators protested in Santiago."

Yemen, Libya, and many other countries are either on the list of countries where unrest has erupted, or are about to join it.

When you analyze the crises in each country, it is easy to see that social, economic, and political injustices are at the bottom of all of them. Yet, these wrongs are nothing new. They have plagued humankind for thousands of years. Why, then, is everyone protesting specifically now, and why is everyone protesting *simultaneously*?

The answers lie in the structure and evolution of human nature. As Jean M. Twenge and W. Keith Campbell beautifully illustrated in *The Narcissism Epidemic: Living in the Age of Entitlement* (Free Press, 2009), people today are not only narcissistic and self-centered, but are becoming more and more so at an alarming rate.

---

116   CNN Wire Staff, "Tear gas flies during Chilean student protests," *CNN* (August 9, 2011), http://edition.cnn.com/2011/WORLD/americas/08/09/chile.protests/index.html

As narcissists, we put ourselves in the center of everything, and "grade" everyone else according to the benefits they may bring us. We connect to the world through the spectacles of self-entitlement. However, this is precisely how we *must not* function if we are to succeed in an era of globalization, when the world is interconnected and interdependent. To succeed, we must want to benefit those to whom we are connected just as much as we wish to benefit ourselves. If we are connected and dependent on each other, then if they are happy, so will we be. And if others are unhappy, we, too, will be unhappy, as demonstrated by Nicholas A. Christakis, MD, PhD, and James H. Fowler, PhD, in *Connected: The Surprising Power of Our Social Networks and How They Shape Our Lives – How Your Friends' Friends' Friends Affect Everything You Feel, Think, and Do.*

The solution, therefore, lies in shifting our viewpoint from self-entitlement to social-entitlement, putting our society first and our egos next, *in order to eventually benefit ourselves.*

In practical terms, this solution entails three goals:

3. Guaranteeing necessary provisions to every member of society.
4. Guaranteeing the continuation of those provisions by inculcating prosocial values into society using mass media and the internet, focusing on the social networks.
5. Using our prosocial work for self-enhancement so we can fully realize the potential that lies within each of us.

To achieve **Goal 1**, an international panel of statespersons, economists, and sociologists representing all the nations, must be set up to devise a plan to establish a just and sustainable economy. Note that the term "just" does not refer to equal distribution of funds or resources (natural or human). Rather, in a just economy no person on earth is left uncared for. Thus, a starving child in Kenya may not need the latest model of iPhone, but is undoubtedly entitled to proper nourishment, a roof over the head, proper education, and proper healthcare.

Conversely, a child of a similar age in Norway may already have the latest iPhone, but still feel miserable to the point of taking his or her own life, or worse yet, that of others, as recent events in that country have shown.[117] The distress in the two cases is very different but just as acute, and both must be addressed by the panel, keeping in mind that, as 2008 Nobel prize laureate and *The New York Times* columnist, Paul Krugman, said, "We are all in the same boat."

Achieving **Goal 2** requires a shift of mindset. Since the media determines the public agenda, it is the media that must lead the way toward annihilating self-centeredness. Instead of the current "Me, me, me," attitude cultivated by the media over the past several decades, its new mottos should be "We, we, we," "mutual guarantee," and "one for all and all for one." If the media describes the benefits of mutual guarantee and the harm in the narcissistic approach, we will naturally gravitate toward sharing and caring, rather than toward suspecting and isolating ourselves. If commercials, infomercials, and infotainments begin to show veneration toward giving individuals, we will all begin to want to give, just as today when the media shows reverence to the rich and powerful, we want to be rich and powerful, as well.

Such a mindset will guarantee that our society remains just and compassionate toward all people, and at the same time that all the people *willingly* contribute to this society. Additionally, many of today's regulating and restraining agencies, such as the police, the army, and financial regulators will either become obsolete or require a fraction of the human and financial resources they currently require. Consequently,

---

117   J. David Goodman, "At Least 80 Dead in Norway Shooting," *The New York Times* (July 22, 2011), http://www.nytimes.com/2011/07/23/world/europe/23oslo.html?pagewanted=all

those resources will be directed toward improving our daily lives, rather than merely toward keeping them relatively safe, with diminishing success.

In such an encouraging and prosocial atmosphere, **Goal 3**, "Using our prosocial work for self-enhancement," will be a natural offshoot. Society will encourage, strive, and *make efforts* to guarantee that each of us realizes his or her personal potential to the maximum, because when that potential is used for the common good, society will benefit. Moreover, liberated from the need to protect ourselves from a hostile environment, a treasure trove of new energies will lend themselves to our self-realization. The result will be eradication of depression and all its related ills, and dramatically enhanced satisfaction from life.

After a few months of living in a society-oriented mindset, we will be baffled by how we could ever have thought that self-interest was a good idea. The evident success and happiness of such a society will yield ever growing motivation to promote and strengthen it, thus creating a perpetual motion in favor of society, and at the same time, in favor of each of its members without neglecting a single one of them.

In our globalized reality, only a form of government that deems the happiness and well-being of *all* the people in the world *equally important* can prove sustainable and successful.

THE ROAD TO SOCIAL JUSTICE

Throughout the world, nations and peoples are awakening, demanding that their governments listen to them, recognize their pain, and resolve their problems. The uproar is not only over food or housing prices. At its base is a firm demand for *social justice*.

Yet, social justice is an elusive goal. With so many sections of society affected by inflation, unemployment, and a lack of education, one person's justice may very well lead to another person's injustice. In the current structure of society, whatever solution is reached, it will only perpetuate, if not exacerbate the current injustice, causing widespread disillusionment, which could trigger more violence or even war.

Thus, the solution to the demand for social justice must involve *all parts of society*, none excluded. The 2011 "Spring of the Nations" proves that the world has changed fundamentally. Humanity has become a single, global entity. As such, it requires that we acknowledge every part of it—both nations and individuals—as worthy in their own right. Nations no longer tolerate occupation, and people no longer tolerate oppression.

If we compare humanity to a human body containing numerous organs of different functions, no organ is redundant. Every organ both contributes what it should to the body, and receives what it needs.

Likewise, the approach to resolving the worldwide unrest must include *all* parts of society. The keywords to all negotiations involving government officials and protesters should be "thoughtful deliberation." The negotiations should be based on the premise that all parties' demands have merit and should be addressed respectfully. Yet, because so many parties have legitimate demands, all parties must take the other parties' demands into account, as well.

In such deliberations, there are no "good guys" or "bad guys." There are people with genuine, legitimate needs, sharing their problems with one another, trying to reach an acceptable, *dignified* solution for all.

Think of a large and loving family. Everyone in the family has his or her needs: Grandpa needs his pills, Dad needs a new suit for his new job, Mom needs her yoga lessons, and brother Ben has just been accepted into a high-priced college. So the family gets together for a family meeting, a bit like Thanksgiving but without the turkey. The members talk about incomes, argue over priorities, share their needs, squabble a bit, and laugh a lot. And in the end, they know what's necessary, what's not, who will get what he or she needs now, and who will get it later. But since they are family, connected by love, those who have to wait agree to wait because after all, they're family.

In many respects, globalization and growing interdependence have turned humanity into a giant-size family. Now we just need to learn how to work as such. If we think about it, a big family is always safer than being alone, provided it functions as a loving family.

Also, we must keep in mind that in almost every country, governments are struggling with mounting deficits and debt. There are not enough resources to go around, but there are certainly enough resources to allow respectable living for all, if only we *acknowledge* each other's needs. Therefore, the "big family way" is the best concept to ensure that social justice is eventually achieved. Just as in a family, the idea is not to break down the system, but to adjust it to cater to people's needs, rather than cater to the desires of various pressure groups.

King Arthur had a round table around which he and his knights would congregate. As its name suggests, the table had no head, implying that everyone who sat there was of equal status. Similarly, governments and citizens need to understand that there is no way to resolve social problems without sitting together at a round table (metaphorically if not physically).

We must remember that we are all mutually responsible for one another and that we are interdependent, like a family. The problems that seem to tackle us around each corner are not the causes, but the *symptoms* of our real problem: lack of solidarity and mutual responsibility for one another. Therefore, it is of utmost importance that we resolve them by calling in the "spirit of the round table."

By resolving these problems one at a time we will gradually build a society governed by mutual guarantee. Indeed, the mindset of mutual guarantee is the real reason we are presented with these problems. Once we achieve mutual guarantee, the problems will be gone like the wind.

TOWARD MUTUAL COMMITMENT

WHY SHARED RESPONSIBILITY IN FACING THE WORLD'S CHALLENGES
IS THE KEY TO RESOLVING THEM IN AN INTERDEPENDENT WORLD

Despite decades of unimaginable efforts, resources, and planning on the part of the UN to eradicate inequality, exploitation, and lack of basic conditions for sustaining life, these problems still pose major challenges in many countries. Around the world, some 1.4 billion people are living on less than $2 a day, while $5.2 billion worth of food are wasted every year in Australia alone.

Jonathan Bloom, author of *American Wasteland: How America Throws Away Nearly Half of Its Food*, writes that "More than 40 percent of the food produced for consumption is wasted by Americans. The total cost of food wasted comes out to an annual amount of more than $100 billion." Worse yet, the gap between those who have and those who have not continues to widen.

For decades, the efforts of developing nations to seek aid in food, health, and development from more affluent countries have been met with highly inadequate results. Until today there was no other choice. After all, the name of the game was "Winner Takes All."

The gaps are not only among countries, but also within them. The sense of deprivation causes both national and international tension, and clearly, given the global crisis, the situation can escalate drastically.

But now the game has changed. The recent emergence of the Spring of Nations is teaching all of us a lesson we should heed carefully: The world is connected, and what goes around comes around. Globalization has made us all interdependent, and no nation can exploit other nations simply because it is stronger, or it will pay dearly. As we can see, countries that yesterday seemed unassailable are crumbling today. They remain solvent only by the mercy of nations that, just a few years back, were treated as inferior.

In today's globalized reality, either we *all* win or we *all* lose, because we are interdependent. When enough people in the world open their eyes to the facts of globalization and shared responsibility, a major shift will begin. No longer will countries and peoples exploit one another; no longer will mammoth consortiums exploit tens of millions of underpaid workers around the world; no longer will children be allowed to die of hunger and illnesses that can be treated with common antibiotics; no longer will women be abused simply because they are women. Indeed, in a world where people realize that their own well-being depends on the well-being of others, they will care for others, who will later care for them in return.

When that shift begins, terms such as "first world" and "third world" will cease to exist. There will be only one world and the people living in it.

CARRYING OUT THE SHIFT

To actualize the above-said, two things are of utmost importance: 1) first aid, 2) education.

By "first aid," we mean that we launch a worldwide campaign that explains why, in a globalized reality, insufficient food supply and lack of clean drinking water are inexcusable and must be corrected without delay. It is easy to show that the cost of such investments pays itself back with interest within a few short years. Countries such as India, Vietnam, and Indonesia serve as wonderful examples, despite all their still existing challenges.

Education means informing people of the new era of globalization, mutual dependence, and shared responsibility, of which we are all part. The recent global financial crises, and the series of uprisings around the world are sufficient evidence that we affect one another on all levels of life—economic, social, and even emotional (see Thomas Friedman's reference to "Globalization of Anger"[118]).

At **Stage One** of the education process, people will realize that it is unthinkable that over a billion people are starving while another billion is throwing away almost half the food it buys and struggles with obesity. Once the bare necessities of life have been provided to the entire world, Stage Two will begin.

Stage Two will focus on enhancing unity and solidarity among individuals and nations, in congruence with the current, interconnected reality.

In Nature, unity, reciprocity, and mutual responsibility are prerequisites to life. No organism survives unless its cells operate in harmony. Likewise, no ecosystem thrives if one of its elements is removed. Until recently, humanity was the only species that did not follow the law of mutual dependence and reciprocity. We believed that Nature's law was "Survival of the Fittest." But now we are beginning to realize that we, too, are subject to interdependence and must play by that rule if we are to survive.

The Campaign

To integrate the messages of mutual responsibility and interdependence, we suggest the following: to declare next year, which the U.N. titled, "The Year of Cooperatives," the starting point of shifting the global mindset toward the urgent need for mutual commitment in order to keep society and economy sustainable.

---

118   Thomas L. Friedman, "A Theory of Everything (Sort Of)," *The York Times* (August 13, 2011), http://www.nytimes.com/2011/08/14/opinion/sunday/Friedman-a-theory-of-everyting-sort-of.html?_r=1

The Steps of the Shift

1. We should assemble an international forum of scientists (from hard sciences as well as social sciences and humanities), artists, thinkers, economists, successful businesspersons, and celebrities under the auspices of the U.N. to declare the start of the Year of Cooperatives. In that conference, the participants will commit to doing their utmost to eradicate hunger and deprivation. They will be chartered by their countries to devise a worldwide campaign to instill the awareness of globalization, shared responsibility, and interdependence.

2. At the end of the forum, teams from the U.N. will work with each country to create media campaigns, school programs, street signs, and other means of advertisement to promote the abovementioned concepts. The goal of the campaign will be to make the idea of exploiting others abominable, and the idea of sharing and caring praiseworthy—and eventually, second nature for us all.

3. The U.N. teams will convene on a regular basis at U.N. headquarters to report on and synchronize their moves, thus promoting uniform global progress toward a sense of mutual responsibility. The teams' meetings will be broadcast live to demonstrate transparency and enhance their credibility. Most important will be the opportunity to show just how productive we can be when we work *together*.

3. Countries, consortiums, and even individuals who excel in demonstrating solidarity and shared responsibility will be praised and glorified, much the same as movie stars and pop stars are admired today. This will be a powerful incentive to encourage those who excel to continue excelling, and to those who are not, to join in.

4. From numerous experiments on the effects of prosocial behavior (such as David W. Johnson and Roger T. Johnson, "An Educational Psychology Success Story: Social Interdependence Theory and Cooperative Learning"[119]), we know that typically Western afflictions such as depression and drug abuse will be all but gone when the campaign takes root. This, in turn, will free up a tremendous amount of financial and human resources to tend to humanity's other needs. International hostilities will also decrease tremendously, even if only for lack of moral and financial support of the adversaries. In an interdependent world, it is simply unwise to battle, and this will be very clear to all.

We at ARI Research have years of experience in international collaborations, networking, and circulation of ideas. We have an online system of free broadcasts simultaneously interpreted into eight languages, and we can produce text and video materials almost at a moment's notice.

We are already collaborating with UNESCO on the topic of global education, and we offer all our services and facilities gratis to the U.N. in hopes of expanding our fruitful partnership.

Today, Nature demands that we unite. Over time, that demand will intensify until we have all consented. At the same time, that demand is the key to our success in building a sustainable reality for ourselves and for our children. In light of all that, we must unite, work together, and we *will* succeed.

---

119   David W. Johnson and Roger T. Johnson, "An Educational Psychology Success Story: Social Interdependence Theory and Cooperative Learning," *Educational Researcher* 38 (2009): 365, doi: 10.3102/0013189X09339057

THE MUTUAL GUARANTEE –
EDUCATIONAL AGENDA

Education is a recognized problem and a painful issue the world over. Uninterested children, declining grades, violence, and disorderly conduct indicate that the education systems in many countries have become dysfunctional.

Some of the problems originate in the structure of the education system and in its inability to adapt to changes. Yet, a change is clearly necessary, particularly because little has changed in schools since their inception back in the days of the Industrial Revolution some 200 years ago. Crowded classrooms, children behind desks, forced to sit still for extended periods of time, short breaks, and vast amounts of useless information to be memorized are still the norm. In the days when schools were first established, there was a genuine need to educate masses of workers to fill the assembly lines.

Thus, the current structure of schools reflects a very narrow perspective of the concept of education. The *Encyclopedia Britannica*, however, defines education in the following way: "Education can be thought of as the transmission of the values and accumulated knowledge of a society. In this sense, it is equivalent to what social scientists term socialization or enculturation. Children—whether conceived among New Guinea tribespeople, the Renaissance Florentines, or the middle classes of Manhattan—are born without culture. Education is designed to guide them in learning a culture, molding their behavior in the ways of adulthood, and directing them toward their eventual role in society."[120]

---

120   "Education," *Encyclopædia Britannica*, http://www.britannica.com/EBchecked/topic/179408/education

Yet, schools today merely aim to equip students with tools by which to continue their schooling at universities and colleges. Schools *do not* educate in the full sense of the word.

Education, as has just been described, is not merely the act of providing knowledge. It is a process for designing the personality and behavior of each of us. Indeed, the essence of education is to teach the student how to cope with and succeed in life. A school that teaches merely how to memorize information is irrelevant in today's reality.

In light of all the above, we have come to realize that we need to make a fundamental change in the educational paradigm. We must examine the challenges that the modern world presents to us and see whether the education we currently provide addresses them sufficiently.

In today's reality, our world has become a global village socially, politically, and economically. From the moment we became attached to one another, we lost the ability to continue leading our lives by values of narcissism and disregard for others. These values may have been useful in the old, individual, and egocentric world, but from the moment humanity turned into an integral, global system, the rules have become identical to those that apply to all integral systems in Nature.

The human body is an example of such an integral system. Within our bodies, the cooperation and harmony (known as homeostasis) among all cells and organs enable the body to maintain proper health. To remain healthy, each cell and organ operates according to the interests of the entire organism. The harmony among the cells turns the healthy body into the astounding machine that it is, and the health of the body contributes, in turn, to the health of each individual cell.

The way the cells in our bodies operate manifests the law of mutual guarantee and reciprocity, which applies to all multilateral connections in Nature. Indeed, the sustainability of the system depends on the reciprocal relations among the elements that comprise it.

Therefore, as long as we continue to relate to one another egoistically, in contrast to the world that has become integral, we act in dissonance with the laws of Nature. In doing so, we are like cells that are parts of an organism, yet consume only for themselves. In the case of the human body, the result of such cells is a cancerous tumor. In the case of humanity, the result is a multilayered, multifaceted global crisis.

To resolve this crisis, we must adjust our network of connections and make it truly global. Each person must recognize the nature of the world we live in, and understand that in the 21st century, one's personal life depends on one's attitude toward others. Therefore, we must educate people to become sensitive toward others, caring, and responsible in their approach to the world.

It follows that in the 21st century, the world needs more than an economic or political solution to its problems. First and foremost, it needs an educational solution.

Numerous studies and books have already determined that the paramount element in the molding of a young person's personality is the surrounding environment.[121] Therefore, to truly "educate" a child means to place him or her in the right environment, one that affects positive results and the right values. To bring up a generation that will annihilate the crises the world is currently experiencing, we must create a different social environment for our children.

---

121 Probably the most notable example of the influence of the social environment on our psyche and even our physical well-being is the book, *Connected: The Surprising Power of Our Social Networks and How They Shape Our Lives – How Your Friends' Friends' Friends Affect Everything You Feel, Think, and Do*, by Nicholas A. Christakis, MD, PhD, and James H. Fowler, PhD (Little, Brown and Co., 2010).

From early on, children need to grow up with the understanding that egoism, the desire to enjoy at the expense of others, is the primary cause of suffering in the adult world. At the same time, we must show children—using various teaching aids—that relationships based on mutual consideration, tolerance, and understanding facilitate harmony and the persistence of life.

TEN KEY PRINCIPLES FOR GLOBAL EDUCATION

1. **The social environment builds the person:** The social environment is the principal element affecting children. Therefore, we must create among them a "miniature society" where everyone cares for everyone else. A child who grows up in such an environment will not only thrive and succeed in expressing his or her creative potential, but will also approach life with a sense of purpose, and with a desire to build a similar society in the "exo-school" environment.

2. **Personal example:** Children learn from the examples we provide them, both personally—from educators and parents—and through the media and other public contents to which they are exposed.

3. **Equality:** During the learning process, there should not be a teacher, but an educator. Although the educator is older in age, he or she will be perceived by the children as "one of them," a peer. In this way, the educator can gradually "pull up" the children in every aspect of the study—informational, as well as moral and social. Thus, for example, during class, children and educators will sit in a circle and talk, with everyone treated as equals.

4. **Teaching through games:** Through games, children grow, learn, and deepen their understanding of how things are connected. A game is a means by which children get to know the world. In fact, children do not learn words by hearing them. Rather, they learn through *experience*. Therefore, it

is necessary to use games as a primary method in working with children. The games should be built in such a way that children will see that they cannot succeed alone, but only with the help of others, that to succeed they must make concessions to others, and that a good social environment can only do them good.

5. **Weekly outings:** Every week there should be a day when the children leave the school and go to a place in the country or some other location, depending on the child's age. Such places can be parks, zoos, factories, farms, movie studios, or theatres. Also, children should be taught how the systems that affect our lives operate, such as the law enforcement, the post office, hospitals, government offices, old-age homes, and any place where children can learn about the processes that are a part of our lives. Before, during, and following the outing, discussions should be held regarding what will be seen, how the experience compared with their expectations, their conclusions, and so forth.

6. **Older teaching the younger:** The older age groups will "adopt" younger groups, while the younger groups will tutor those who are younger still. In this way, everyone feels part of the learning process and acquires necessary tools for communicating with others.

7. **"Little court":** As part of the learning process, children should act out situations that they encounter in their daily lives: envy, power struggles, deceit, and so on. After acting them out, they should try to scrutinize them. Through such experiences, children will learn to understand and be sensitive to others. They will comprehend that others can be in the right, too, even if they cannot accept their views at the moment. They will see that tomorrow they might find themselves in a similar situation, that every person and every

view has its place in the world, and that everyone should be treated with tolerance.

8. **Video taping activities:** It is recommended that all activities be videotaped for later viewing and analysis together with the children. In this way, children will be able to see how they reacted or behaved in certain situations. They will be able to analyze the changes they are going through and develop the ability to introspect.

9. **Small groups with several educators:** It is highly recommended that each group of 10 students has a team of two educators and a supporting professional (a psychologist).

10. **Parent support:** The parents must support the educational process unfolding at school. They should talk to the children about the importance of the values inculcated at school, set a personal example of these values in their behavior, and completely avoid instilling other values. To facilitate this, there should also be courses for parents.

COLLABORATION WITH UNESCO

The method of global education has been warmly accepted by the Director-General of UNESCO, Mrs. Irina Bokova. At the moment, a UNESCO-ARI joint book on global education is in the making, and a series of international conferences and meetings has taken place and is planned for the future.

FURTHER READING

The Psychology of the Integral Society

The Psychology of the Integral Society presents a revolutionary approach to education. In an interconnected and interdependent world, teaching children to compete with their peers is as "wise" as teaching one's left hand to outsmart the right hand. An integral society is one in which all the parts contribute to the well-being and success of society. Society, in turn, is responsible for the well-being and success of those within it, thus forming interdependence. In a globalized, integrated world, this is the only sensible and *sustainable* way to live.

In this book, a series of dialogs between professors Michael Laitman and Anatoly Ulianov sheds light on the principles of an eye-opening approach to education. Absence of competition, child rearing through the social environment, peer equality, rewarding the givers, and a dynamic makeup of group and instructors are only some of the new concepts introduced in this book. *The Psychology of the Integral Society* is a must-have for all who wish to become better parents, better teachers, and better persons in the integrated reality of the 21st century.

"What's expressed in *The Psychology of the Integral Society* should get people thinking about other possibilities. In solving any difficult problem, all perspectives need to be explored. We spend so much time competing and trying to get a leg up that the concept of simply working together sounds groundbreaking in itself."

~Peter Croatto, *ForeWord Magazine*

A Guide to the New World: why mutual guarantee is the key to our recovery from the global crisis

Why does 1% of the world population own 40% of the wealth? Why are education systems throughout the world producing unhappy, poorly educated children? Why is there hunger? Why are food prices rising when there is more than enough food for everyone? Why are there still countries where human dignity and social justice are nonexistent? And when and how will these wrongs be made right?

In 2011, these questions touched the hearts of hundreds of millions the world over. The cry for social justice has become a demand around which all can unite. We all long for a society where we can feel safe, trust our neighbors, and guarantee the future of our children. In such a society, all will care for all, and mutual guarantee—where all are guarantors of each other's well-being—will thrive.

Despite all the challenges, we believe that change is possible and that we can find a way to implement it. Therefore, the book you are holding in your hands is a positive, *optimistic* one.

We now have a unique opportunity to achieve global transformation in a peaceful, pleasant manner, and A *Guide to the New World* tries to help us pave the way toward that goal.

The book is divided into two parts, plus indices. Part One contains the concept of mutual guarantee. Part Two details the building of the new mutual guarantee society, and recaps the principles presented in Part One. The indices contain previous publications of the ARI Institute detailing its social, educational, and economic ideologies.

ABOUT THE ARI INSTITUTE

MISSION STATEMENT

The Advanced Research of Integration (ARI) Institute is a 501(c) (3) nonprofit organization dedicated to promoting positive changes in educational policies and practices through innovative ideas and solutions. These can be applied to the most pressing educational issues of our time. The ARI Institute introduces a new way of thinking by explaining the benefits of recognizing and implementing the new rules humanity needs to succeed in an interdependent, integrated world.

Through its networks, activities and multimedia resources, ARI Institute promotes international and interdisciplinary cooperation.

WHAT WE DO

We encourage active dialogue on the global crisis as an opportunity to facilitate a positive shift in global thinking about educating future generations, thus enabling them to cope with massive shifts in climate, economics, and geopolitical relations. Our materials are free and available to all, regardless of age, gender, religion, political, or cultural considerations.

The materials reveal the integral, global system of natural laws manifesting in society today. We are committed to sharing our knowledge on an international level through our established multimedia channels. We are further committed to enhancing people's awareness of the need to conduct their relations in a spirit of mutual responsibility and personal involvement.

OUR VALUES

We are all living in trying times, confronted by personal, environmental, and social crises. These crises are occurring because humankind has been unable to perceive the interconnectedness and interdependence among us and between the human race and Nature. By providing information to the public through a rich media environment, we act as a catalyst to shift human behavior toward a more sustainable model. We advocate a solution to the current global crisis and promote it through our unique educational content, presented via media channels worldwide.

Through extensive research and public activities, ARI Institute offers a clear, coherent understanding of the natural development of the events and societal degradation that have led to the current state of affairs in our global, integral world. Additionally, we are expanding our online environment to reach children. They will benefit by participating in an educational process that encourages them to become tolerant, responsible, and considerate human beings living as global citizens.

In this internet-based environment, children will collaborate in activities simultaneously occurring in different parts of the world. Such activities will help them recognize that they are all connected within a united global village, and show them how they can help improve humanity by participating in these programs. We believe that exposure to this environment can profoundly change an entire generation of children, turning them into responsible citizens of the world, and marking a turning point in humankind's currently destructive behaviors.

WHERE WE STAND ON EDUCATION

The new generation is facing a completely new world filled with unprecedented challenges. If we focus on our children's needs, we can significantly help them face problems such as drug abuse, violence, and increasing school dropout rates, issues that we believe are not being successfully addressed by most current educational systems.

WHERE WE STAND ON ECONOMICS

The crisis is neither financial nor economic, nor is it ecological. Rather, it is a global crisis that encompasses our entire civilization and all realms of life. Therefore, we must look at the root of it and address the common cause—our self-centered nature.

We believe that a superficial change in society will not yield a lasting solution. First, we must alter the connections between us, moving from egocentrism to altruism. This is the principle by which integral systems operate, and today we are discovering that human society is precisely such a system.

OUR ACTIVITIES

TV and Video Productions

ARI Films (www.arifilms.tv) is ARI's film and television department, a highly successful, dynamic production enterprise specializing in content for the Internet, cable, and satellite television stations. ARI Films produces educational and documentary programs, docudramas, and talk show series, as well as custom made productions. The ARI Films team consists of experienced professionals from a wide array of fields including video editors, animators, cameramen, scriptwriters, producers and directors.

International Forums

ARI organizes regular international forums all over the world that are attended by large audiences eager to participate in its lectures and workshops. These forums are broadcast live over the internet and on cable and satellite TV networks.

The Citizens of the Future:
Our Education Center and Network

Citizens of the Future is a not-for-profit educational association established under the auspices of ARI. It aims to provide children, youth, and parents with an online learning environment that promotes values of love and caring for others, so vital in this global age. We believe that children who acquire and adhere to these values will be well positioned for a life of happiness, joy, and self-fulfillment. To achieve its goals, the Citizens of the Future association operates on several levels, as listed below.

Network of Children's Education Centers

Citizens of the Future education centers are places where the method of "building human beings" is developed and implemented on a daily basis. Here, a loving and supportive environment is constructed in favor of the children, based on friendship and care for each other. The activities include:

- Activities and games that promote bonding among the children;
- Discussions about Nature in general and human nature in particular;
- Complementary lessons on various school topics;
- Developing the necessary social skills for interpersonal and group communication;
- Outings to museums, parks, nature reserves, courthouses, and many more locations and facilities that help introduce the children to the systems that affect our lives;
- Documentation of activities and preparation of structured tutorials for instructors to circulate this innovative method worldwide.

YFU Youth Movement

The youth movement, YFU (Youth For Unity), was specifically formed to create a supportive, loving environment for youths from 12-18 who aspire to promote the values of mutual consideration and love of others. This social framework is a direct extension of the complementary education center, Citizens of the Future.

Activities of YFU include:

- Studies of Nature in general and human nature in particular;
- Professional training;
- Cinema school;
- Conventions, trips, and other unity-promoting activities;
- Tutoring and training of children, to qualify the next generation for life in an interconnected world;
- Preparation and guidance for life as adults in today's world;
- Developing lesson plans on love of others, human nature, and Nature as a whole;
- Production and distribution of children's programs and programs on education;
- Developing educational games;
- Organizing conventions for children, parents, and educators.

ABOUT DR. MICHAEL LAITMAN, FOUNDER OF THE ARI INSTITUTE

Dr. Laitman is the highly qualified founder of the ARI Institute. He holds degrees as Professor of Ontology and Theory of Knowledge, a PhD in Philosophy, and an MS in Medical Cybernetics. Today, the ARI Institute has branches throughout North America, Central and South America, as well as Asia, Africa, and Western and Eastern Europe.

Dr. Laitman is dedicated to discovering and promoting positive changes in educational policies and practices, and applying them to the most pressing educational problems of our time. He proposes a new approach to education that implements the rules of living in an interdependent, integrated world.

A Guide to Living in a Globalized World

Dr. Laitman provides specific guidelines for how to live in the new global village, our increasingly technologically interconnected world. His fresh perspective touches all areas of human life: social, economic, and environmental, with a particular emphasis on education. He outlines a new global education system based on universal values. This would create a cohesive society in our emerging, more tightly interconnected reality.

In his meetings with Mrs. Irina Bokova, Director-General of UNESCO, and with Dr. Asha-Rose Migiro, Deputy Secretary-General of the UN, he discussed current worldwide education problems and his vision for their solution. This crucial topic is presently in the process of major transformation. Dr. Laitman stresses the urgency of taking advantage of newly available communication tools, while considering the unique aspirations of today's youth and preparing them for life in a highly dynamic, global world.

In recent years Dr. Laitman has worked closely with many international institutions and has participated in several international events in Tokyo with the Goi Peace Foundation, Arosa (Switzerland), and Düsseldorf (Germany), and with the International Forum of Cultures in Monterrey (Mexico). These events were organized with the support of UNESCO. In these global forums, he contributed to vital discussions concerning the world crisis, and outlined the steps required to create positive change through an enhanced global awareness.

Dr. Laitman has been featured in international media, including *Corriere della Sera*, the *Chicago Tribune*, the *Miami Herald*, *The Jerusalem Post*, and *The Globe* and on RAI TV and Bloomberg TV.

He has devoted his life to exploring human nature and society, seeking answers to the meaning of life in our modern world. The combination of his academic background and extensive knowledge make him a sought-after world thinker and speaker. Dr. Laitman has written over 40 books that have been translated into 18 languages, all with the goal of helping individuals achieve harmony among them and with the environment around them.

Dr. Laitman's scientific approach allows people of all backgrounds, nationalities, and faiths to rise above their differences and unite around the global message of mutual responsibility and collaboration.

CONTACT INFORMATION

Inquiries and general information:
info@ariresearch.org

USA
2009 85th St., Suite 51
Brooklyn NY, USA -11214
Tel. +1-917-6284343

Canada
1057 Steeles Avenue West
Suite 532
Toronto, ON – M2R 3X1 Canada
Tel. +1 416 274 7287

Israel
112 Jabotinsky St.,
Petach Tikva, 49517 Israel
i.vinokur@ariresearch.org
Tel. +972-545606780

And See What Happens

For Chris, for Roy.
For Lyn, Elizabeth and Mary
for David and for Dirk
for Glenn and for Gordon—
darling companions

Contents

One: And See What Happens

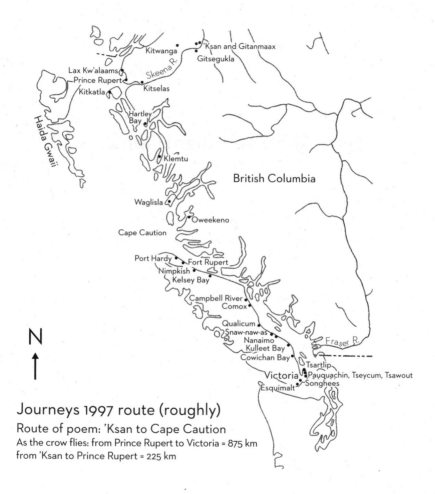

Kitwanga

'Ksan and Gitanmaax

Gitsegukla

Skeena R.

Lax Kw'alaams
Prince Rupert
Kitkatla

Kitselas

Hartley
Bay

Haida Gwaii

Klemtu

British Columbia

Waglisla

Oweekeno

Cape Caution

Port Hardy
Fort Rupert
Nimpkish
Kelsey Bay

Campbell River
Comox

Qualicum
Snaw-naw-as
Nanaimo
Kulleet Bay
Cowichan Bay

Fraser R.

Tsartlip
Pauquachin, Tseycum, Tsawout
Victoria
Songhees
Esquimalt

N

↑

Journeys 1997 route (roughly)

Route of poem: 'Ksan to Cape Caution
As the crow flies: from Prince Rupert to Victoria = 875 km
from 'Ksan to Prince Rupert = 225 km

And See What Happens
Notes from Vision Quest: Journeys 1997, a thirty-day, thousand-
mile paddle in a Coast Salish canoe

Guarantee you'll be a different person. Take Kleenex, you will need it.
                                                              —Frank Nelson

Prologue

February 4, 1997
Vancouver RCMP Division "E" HQ
Aboriginal Policing

They have gathered together from all over BC. Men and women, RCMP members and members of the First Nations, young and old. Many whose hearts are hardened. Many on both sides whose anger reaches to the marrow. Warriors, healers, teachers, visionaries, *dreamers* all, they are volunteers for a journey whose purpose is to communicate the desire for community. A journey that will raise the hope of recovering from addictions. A journey too arduous for mere muscle and skill, a spiritual voyage that if successful will draw a healing circle one thousand miles in diameter on the map of the coast.

Vision quest

Step in, it is time.
Our canoe is strong enough

to bear our burden
yet so frail we'll have to sweat

and blister and bleed
to keep her afloat. We will navigate

the salty rivers
to our own dark heart.

We must find what we need
to bring us back home.

How do you begin to build community?

We are being destroyed, especially our young adults.
We are facing the fight of our lives.

—Ken Innes

Thirty days to pull a thousand miles
white water, wind
currents, tides

and dangerous crossings.
A thousand miles
from 'Ksan, on the flood-swollen Skeena,

to Victoria of the beautiful name, Mituli.
A thousand miles to pull
Nunsulsailus (Many Hands)

Skookum Kalitin (Strong Arrow)
and *L 'Swiet* (Soul Entering).
In each space of thirty-one feet

by four-and-a-half feet,
nine pullers must strain and sweat
and sing and laugh and cry together

and argue and fight and fall silent.
And see what happens.

The grandfathers' journey

has not been done by canoe in a hundred years.
That is because the knowledge and the will

to build those canoes were long ago smashed
by Mounties made to do the government's dirty work.

They burned the longhouses and the regalia
and the art of ritual, arrested those who potlatched,

dragged children out of their homes to the residential schools,
leaving fathers and mothers with no reason to carry on.

At each community the RCMP will sit still,
have their sins named by grandmothers,

by grandfathers, by parents of teen suicides,
by the children peeking out from the chiefs' robes.

Then Inspector John Grant, hardened veteran,
poet and brave man, will stand and apologize for

"those acts which, although sanctioned
by law at the time, were morally wrong."

After that, the pullers are promised,
there will be feasting.

Gitanmaax
'Ksan

Gitsegukla
Kitwanga

Kitselas
Prince Rupert

Lax Kw'alaams
Kitkatla

Hartley Bay
Klemtu

Waglisla
Oweekeno

Port Hardy
Fort Rupert

Nimpkish
Kelsey Bay

Campbell River
Comox

Qualicum
Snaw-naw-as

Nanaimo
Kulleet Bay

Cowichan Bay
Tsartlip

Pauquachin
Tseycum

Tsawout
Songhees

Esquimalt
Victoria

Teacher, visionary, healer, warrior

Skipper Roy Henry Vickers, a powerful visionary determined to bring the message of healing to every addict in Canada, intends to raise enough funds to build an addictions recovery centre in BC, one open to all nations, all colours, all faiths. Since 90 percent of policing is necessary only because of addictions, Inspector John Grant wonders why no one has ever had such an idea before. If we are successful, he says, we will have put ourselves out of a job. As a young man Vickers dreamed of joining the RCMP but was turned down because he was colour-blind. So, he became an artist.

Sweat lodge

We sit in darkness so we can look at ourselves.
We sit on the ground to remind us where we come from.
We sit in a circle to remind us everything we do comes back to us.

—Traditional

(for John Elliott)

This is what I see from my place
in the circle in the Turtle Lodge:
a man of prayer
laying red-hot grandfather stones

in a hole dug four hundred years deep
to the dirt of Turtle Island. I am
ashamed of my white skin standing in
for the murderers of ritual—

how can I endure his blessing?
Then he seals the door and I see
nothing. He instructs us to pray
for strength and courage

but I am unable to remember
a single word of prayer.
At the first rush of steam
I remember white water

boiling on the Thompson,
a bridge pier steaming upriver
as we chased it to build our strength.
Another burst of steam—

the ground lurches under me,
someone shouts, the bridge flies
across the sky and *Holy Mary
Mother of God, pray for us sinners . . .*

We learn to pray after
white-water practice on the Thompson

High in the sage hills above the Thompson
a campfire crackles. We relax
in the rich, silent afterglow of danger
met and faced. Everyone is warm

and dry and fed; the stories have been told.
The pines surround us standing
black against the blue night sky,
the burning stars.

Steven picks up his guitar,
begins to strum the song
gifted us by Frances Paul,
elder of the Tsartlip people:

Hi Ni-Ni O Hi Ni-Ni O
Hi O Hi O Hi O Way

We stand, join hands and sing.
As the last note fades,
for one long, graceful moment
we forget to let go.

The journey is over before it begins

In the odd way
the white man sometimes has,
the journey is completed
before it is begun—
one thousand miles by bus
from Victoria to 'Ksan.
Many days and many miles later,
in Qualicum,
the Mounties will be teased
even as they are congratulated
on their canoeing skills:
It's nice to paddle and enjoy
the scenery as you go. Used to be
the white man comes along
in his little boat
and paddles backward.

Finding the inner strength to deal with pain and fatigue brings up personal issues

(for Leslie Marrion, for David Payne,
for Ed Hill)

You won't hear anyone complain
about blackflies. Sunburn. The fact that someone
is hoarding the sunscreen. And the deet.

Or about dehydration. Blisters.
Back pain. Neck pain. Unrelenting.

No one gets cranky.

A full day's paddle, bed by 1:00 if the speeches go long.
Up by 4:00 to catch the morning tide.
Sleep deprivation days on end.

Rain and wind and spray and sweat.
Soaked to the skin, shaking, blue lips, numb feet—
just climb up the seiner's cargo net, dry out
in the engine room. Put dry clothes on and get back at it.

No one whines about hauling camping gear
over slippery rocks after dark. If the cookhouse
isn't set up, at least the cooking angels
are making emergency stew on the seiner.

No one grumbles if gear was scattered
by other crews rummaging around.
If a sleeping bag is wet. Not even if someone else
is sleeping in it and can't be found.

In fact the recording of bagpipes echoing full blast
in the net loft at Namu at 7:00 a.m., taking full advantage
of the wonderful acoustics, tempts not one person
to use profanity, though I can't say if it lifts anyone's spirits.

Then one day lunch is ham and cheese sandwiches
one too many times and all of a sudden
there is a plan to jump ship in Campbell River.

'Ksan, the arrival

At 'Ksan the totem poles face water
ready to greet the great canoes.
After four generations of waiting
how astonished they must have been

to see us. The totems at Kitwanga
missed our arrival. Tired
of waiting, they had turned
to face the railroad. Along the banks

of the Skeena the old women
weep at a sight they have not
seen since childhood. They stand, silent
raise their hands as we pass.

The policemen bear the burden of the chief's esteem on their shoulders

Roy Henry Vickers sits in the stern of Nunsulsailus,
clad in full regalia, serene, as the RCMP,
sweating in red serge, pull him into the bay.

As the canoe nears shore, he stands
and they strain to keep him steady, to do him proud,
to give him a landing worthy of a chief.

He addresses the crowd, begins to holler his request
for permission to land: "Honoured chiefs, elders,
women of high rank, our precious children:

We have come a long way ..."

How many embraces can a humble man endure?

We welcome you to our shores. Come up, come up;
the fire is burning, the cooking is done, the carpet is laid for you.
—Traditional

The people sing us in to shore
and we respond by singing.
Drummers accompany us to the great hall
where children take our hands and lead us
to fancy tables, to sideboards bent with food.

The chiefs admit dismay at the sight
of so many uniforms in town,
but respect for our difficult journey,
for the sacrifice of time away from families.
We thank you for what you are doing.

Then we hear from the people
who still hear screams echo from the halls
of the residential schools, who still cry
every night for their lost families.
We welcome you with joy for what you are doing.

When John Grant stands up for his ritual apology,
his words quiver like the small muscles
of an arm that carries too much weight.
The words the people hear do not at all match
the formal speech his lips are trying to shape.

They hear: *We are sorry.*

Then we must dance. Having no nation
of our own, we are named Butterflies.
We dance around children doing the
Blanket Dance to catch cash tossed
for the recovery centre fund.

The policemen are completely undone.
Some of them are weeping.
Some of them have loosened buttons and belts.
Some of them wear beads over their red serge.
Children have sweet-talked them
into letting them wear their Stetsons.

Trays of dessert come around, and come around
and come around again, offered by children
who will not take no for an answer.

The menu at Kitkatla

geoduck   seal   braided seal organs
    clam fritters   dried seaweed
        smoked Alaska black cod
          seaweed with roe
       roe on hemlock branches
chow mein   octopus   king crab
    fried oysters   baked oysters
       fried sea cucumbers
baked sea cucumbers   smoked salmon
    poached salmon   baked salmon
deer soup   deer meat   cold cuts
      bannock   baked bread
      raw vegetables with dip
  five different salads   six rice dishes
    four pastas   three kinds of pie
     three cakes   cookies and tarts

Tskgeegany

(for Cecil Hill)

Tskgeegany was the traditional summer home of Kitkatla people, long abandoned to moss and fern—a hushed place, a sacred place, a place where *the grandmothers and grandfathers still walk*. Illegal loggers dynamited a road through the gravesite and flung boulders across the creek into the village, leaving holes in the air and in the ground: absences that cannot be filled.

The elders are dying

(for Rita Robertson and Esther Shackelly)

All along the coast the elder women teach
their daughters and granddaughters to dance.
For five years or so now those young women

have been learning the steps and words to songs
that have not been performed in four generations.

Where do these songs come from?
Rita says, *I just close my eyes and they come.*

The *grandmothers and grandfathers*
know when it is time and they help the memories come.

At the table, at the campfire, in a rafted-up canoe, young hands
are busy sewing regalia, comparing stitches, sharing buttons.

The elders are dying of that which defines them.
There is so little time left to remember. In the bighouse

dancers circle counter-clockwise
to slow time down.

The communities apologize, one after the other

(for Hartley Bay)

We welcome you, but we apologize because we are not so cheerful—
we are suffering from the death of a fifteen-year-old from suicide. In
our language we have a saying when something like this happens.
It sums it all up. I know you pullers will understand us now. When
someone in our community dies we say, *Our canoe has overturned.*

The word for policeman

(for Elaine Assu Price)

In the course of her research, a young student named Elaine Price discovers that among the many languages of the west coast, the word policeman always translates roughly the same—to "the man who takes you away." Not "the man you call when you are afraid," or "the man you go to when you are lost," but *the man who takes you away*. Elaine's mother was a child in the days when *singing and dancing* were punishable by imprisonment. In her old age, she came to visit Elaine in New Aiyansh. She spent most of the time in the bedroom with the lights turned off, but finally asked Elaine whether the people of this town were really so bad. She saw so many policemen, and at night they always parked their car next door.

William teaches the pullers some fun dances

(for William Wasden)

In this one, he says, you dance around the circle,
two by two. When you hear the drum beat change,

one of you pretends to kill the other with a lance,
while he tries to duck away.

Then you switch sides because sometimes
you win and sometimes you lose.

Then for a while you dance together in peace,
because you can't fight all the time.

The singers

A camera flash at Open Bight captures Lloyd, Shaun and Barry, rapt faces against a black sky, as they huddle together on a log. Flashlights illuminate the pages of a songbook. *Do you remember when / we used to sing: Sha la la la la la la la la la te da.* One of the kids from the Bella Bella canoe taps Shaun on the shoulder. "Are you guys high?"

Nunsulsailus falls under a spell

We break stride.
Nunsulsailus wallows, settles deep.
The paddlers jab at the water,
each one straining
to pull her whole weight.
A murmur grows, grows ugly:

He's the one … never should have … his fault…
that one, too … lily-dipping …

Shh, Chris says,
shhh and shhh.
Listen to what you are saying.

Shh,
Listen to what you are saying.

Shh, shh, shh,
Listen.

Shh … listen

We all listen
until there is nothing left to hear.

With one breath we dig our paddles in.
Nunsulsailus lifts up, takes off.
We fly for miles
all the way to shore
where just in time
someone shouts, breaks the spell,
sets us safely down.

The skipper warns us
that tomorrow will not be a picnic

Remember your paddle is made of a living tree.
A tree that has been thanked. When you are very tired
or very frightened, pray to it. It will help you.
—Traditional

Tomorrow we round Cape Caution,
Roy says. You can forget everything

you've experienced up to this point.
Tomorrow the wind and the ocean

will take everything you have
and you will have to reach deep

inside for more and if you can't find it
we are going to be in a lot of trouble.

I lie in bed shaking, the morning tide
only a few hours away.

I am asking myself a question.

Cape Caution and the spiritual canoe

You are learning to paddle the spiritual canoe,
the canoe you paddle every day of your life.

—Traditional

Roy knows it is time. He heads
straight out into the wilderness
while the coast guard hollers
over the radio to get closer in
and I pray to my paddle the living tree.
How can I ground myself
in twelve-foot swells, the pitching
horizon? Instead, I think of geese and grace,
and all around us, grey whales spout.

I am here; my paddle is wet.

Five hours of hard pulling.
When I have nothing left, I reach out
to my seatmate. Sing me a song,
Chris, or tell me again about
jumping mouse who gave away

his eyes so he could *see*
the sacred mountains. And we all sing
for each other—my crewmates
are the burden I carry while I ride
for free on their shoulders. And we all

cling, blind, to the neck feathers
of Nunsulsailus as she flies
up each peak and descends
in joyous thirty-foot swoops until
we gently touch down on shore.

The final apology

Gilakas'la means thank you. It also means hello.

Hi Ni-Ni O Hi Ni-Ni O
Hi O Hi O Hi O Way

We are sorry
it took us this long
to visit.

Two: Frog River

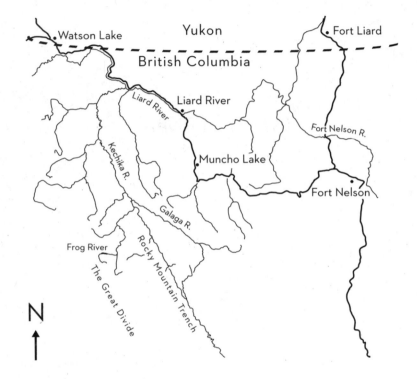

Watson Lake
Yukon
Fort Liard
British Columbia
Liard River
Liard River
Kechika R.
Muncho Lake
Fort Nelson R.
Galaga R.
Fort Nelson
Frog River
Rocky Mountain Trench
The Great Divide

N

Frog River (roughly)
Northern Rockies
From Muncho Lake to Frog River flight = 128 km.

Frog River
Notes from an outpost cabin in the northern Rockies

Love is so difficult, like horse-racing, like fog.
                    —Sean Penn in *She's So Lovely*

I

A heck of a wind
bounces me into the mountains.

You, back in your garden,
your small scrap of sky.

A ridge narrows to a knife edge—
the Cessna teeters along.

Our shadow tumbles into a cirque.
Mountain goats, unperturbed.

We could fall from the sky.
We could grow feathers.

II

Sleeping bag, backpack, gas for the outboard.
The Cessna bobs obediently on its rope.

The river: two sides, divided.
Did I leave you—or leave you behind?

Silence: at first it's all I hear.
Next I hear what I imagined.

No bear repellent for sale in Fort Nelson—
only attractants: scented cherry, and honey.

Four degrees in the cabin.
Chopping block, axe: let the chips fly!

III

I dropped my pencil into the river—dark ripple
all that is left of the word *love*.

Goddam hissing lamp swings from its nail.
Makes shadows move.

Propane is not good to write poems by.
A candle is better, or darkness.

I see a mouse has been busy:
he's left a message in the frying pan.

May I use your line
about the best of intentions?

IV

Rain drums on the tin roof.
Mice skitter in the drawer; fine by me.

Me in my sleeping bag,
you on your Posturepedic.

The wood stove—
could you comfort me as well?

How can I sleep in such darkness?
I close my eyes—no difference.

Your big paw on my breast
even here.

V

Two degrees below in the cabin.
Ice on shore. A tentative morning.

Freeze-dried coffee with Coffee-mate.
You've no idea how delicious.

The red canoe gleams
in its bed of moss and pine.

Wild cranberries in my porridge.
After a freeze, they taste much sweeter.

The last raspberries still cling,
 colour of bruised lips.

VI

Perfectly still, river becomes mountain
becomes cloud.

Canoe becomes bird,
the hollow bone.

I am afraid to look down—
vertigo and the belly's lurch!

I remember your cheek against mine,
a held breath.

Have I mentioned
I could fall?

VII

I fish all day for one fish.
I am learning the meaning of desire.

This knife will not penetrate.
Slippery fish! Hold still!

How did the mouse
get in the trout's stomach?

Cranberries, the red canoe,
blood on the stone.

Poor fish, I butchered you.
I wish I had killed you beautifully.

VIII

I cast my line out
every day.

Blood on my thumb—
I am hooked.

There is no end to love,
like perfume, like kissing.

Is that a fish?
Or a drop of rain?

Which is better?
The desire, or the touch?

IX

Hotdogs, marshmallows, beer, beans.
I am an old-fashioned camper.

Grizzly bear tracks by the outhouse.
Should I leave the door open or closed?

Learn to read a bear's intention
by his behaviour.

They say a man's heart breaks more easily
than a woman's, no matter his bluster.

This is dangerous country.
They say don't go in unarmed.

X

Three things I need to survive:
fish hook, axe, knife.

Since we are counting,
where are you?

I remember you slicing tomatoes,
your thumbs testing for ripeness.

I am getting quite good with the axe—
aim for the chopping block, not the stick.

Your big hands, your scarred thumb.
Knives must be sharp, you said, sharpening mine.

XI

Chop wood
Haul water

Chop wood
Haul water

Chop wood
Haul water

Chop wood
Haul water

Chop wood
Haul water

XII

After frost the underbrush burns:
orange buckbrush, red bunchberry.

I press plants in these pages: kinnikinnick,
blueberry, avens, star moss.

Fringed fleabane. Woolly lousewort.
Cursed crowfoot. Bastard toadflax.

Is one word more beautiful than another?
I paddle for miles. What for? Another tree?

I have been drunk on pine all day.
Time for a beer.

XIII

The single barbless hook.
Why so much blood?

I am getting better at paddling alone:
only a little zigzag.

The loon calls and dives and calls and dives
and calls and dives again.

Wouldn't you know it, tacked to the wall,
a hand-drawn map to the great divide.

I watch snow fall on the river
until my lips are numb.

XIV

Piles of scat bristle with hair.
What do I do now?

On this trail—a moose,
a grizzly, a hunter, me.

Shout, keep still, shout, keep still, shout, keep still.
It is all so confusing.

The tongue hardens around a word.
A stone, softened in the mouth will speak.

Did I say I was lost?
I probably lied.

XV

A gunshot.
Someone has killed that which he desires.

Downstream, a grizzly
stands up to taste the air.

Love is so dangerous:
the bared throat.

A mouse runs like hell along shore.
Be careful! I want to call out.

Someone has flagged the trail.
Lucky for me.

XVI

The great divide:
Frog to the Arctic, Goose to the Pacific.

Why speak of destinations?
Have I not just arrived?

A tear falls.
From here it could go either way.

Only fog flows uphill.
Love is so complicated.

These notes—
good for starting fires.

XVII

The poem I hung in the cabin window
has faded.

The Cessna bounces
down to the river.

Sleeping bag, backpack,
knife and axe.

I am out of paper. I brush
my footprints from the sand on shore.

Whisky Jack, Crow:
what have I stolen?

Notes to the Poems:

"There is no end to love ..." and "Love is so difficult" in the epigraph and in VIII are from the film *She's So Lovely*, written by John Cassavetes.

"I cast my line out ..." in VIII: this idea came from Carra Noelle.

"drunk on pine" in XII is from Pablo Neruda.

I thank Lorna Crozier for what I learned from her book *Bones in Their Wings*.

Three: Last One to Get There

Cape Sutil

Experiment Bight

Cape Scott →

Goletas Channel

Duval Island

San Josef Bay →
Cape Palmerston →

Port Hardy

Grant Bay
Cape Parkins

← Quatsino Sound

Keith River

Lawn Point

Ambrosia Bay →

Cape Cook →

Solander Island

Brooks Peninsula

McLean Island →

Zeballos

Kapoose Creek →

Grassy Island

Tatchu Point

Little Espinosa Inlet

N

Northern Vancouver Island (roughly)
As the crow flies: from Cape Scott to Zeballos = 150 km

Last One to Get There

Notes from a twenty-two-day kayaking trip from Port Hardy
to Zeballos on northern Vancouver Island

Launching is far simpler than landing.

—John Kimantas

Duval Island

Pinned down.
Blown off the water early the first day out.
The only safe scrap of bouldered beach is across from a fish camp.
A couple of guys motor over and ask do we need anything.
Sniffing around for *younger* women.
They roar back to camp.
Mosquitoes move in.

Goletas

Whales in the channel!
We peel out and give chase.
Too late—just distant spouts and the faint stink of fish.
Once again we paddle along shore like ducklings following Glenn.
Off John's stern a minke eye emerges and takes a long look.
Whale! I call—too late, it's gone.

Cape Sutil

I'm getting too old for this.
Every muscle aches, my palms are blistered.
Don't know what made me think I was in shape.
Cape Sutil is the most northerly point on the Island.
I guess that means it's all downhill from here.
The petroglyphs stare out to sea.
Eyes open wide.

Experiment Bight

Two a.m. and a maniac wind howls.
A hell-driver on the freeway at midnight.
I cover my ears and wait for it to slam into us.
I say holy mother of god Lyn get your camera ready.
We'll be the first two women to round Cape Scott in a tent.
We'll make a fortune on the book tour.
If we survive.

Cape Scott

We have optimum conditions.
Sea rippled with wind and tide at our backs.
Only mountains to climb—a four-metre haul to the top of each swell.
I need to remember to watch my speed coming down.
Kayaks appear, disappear, appear, disappear.
Dear mother of god help me calm down.
We do have optimum conditions.

San Josef Bay

I have no dry clothes left.
After days of rain it rains again.
It rains right through my raingear.
It rains so hard my dry bags get wet.
The cockpit cover doesn't stop it; I have to bail.
I swear it rains so hard the water looks like velvet.
And we heave up and down on a billowing sea.

Cape Palmerston

A rock-strewn hard surf landing.
Too hungry and cold and tired to wonder how we'll get off again.
Next morning the sun breaks through to dry us out.
We festoon beach logs with bras and panties.
The creek spills tea into the sea.
Cedar water.
Ahhhh.

Grant Bay

The sand shimmers.
I think of thatched huts.
Beach chairs, waiters, margaritas.
Pineapples, cocktail umbrellas, cerveza por favor!
A mariachi band winding its way through.
But we have none of that at Grant Bay.
Thank god.

Cape Parkins

Up at 4:30, away by 6:10.
We launched too early this morning.
The wind still howls down Quatsino Sound.
In an instant we are flung apart, scattered wide.
Lyn and I fight for ground against the thundering headwind.
We are the last to reach shelter behind the lighthouse.
Where the others are already fishing.

Lawn Point

No, that can't be right—we're not going in there!
Glenn aims for the narrow gap between shore and a line of reefs.
One by one we thread the minefield that guards Lawn Point.
A roaring wall of water crashes down just behind me.
It lifts and scoots the kayak through the gap.
Then we have lunch on the lawn.
Quite civilized, really.

Keith River

Sunday.
We hop the small surf over the bar.
The river draws us in to its still corridors.
Rainforest, hung with moss and green light.
So silent we dare not talk or splash our paddles.
An eagle sits on a snag just over our heads.
He turns, looks the other way.

Ambrosia Beach

A perilous crossing.
The wind builds at Solander.
Brooks Bay kicks us around with three-metre swells and haystacks.
Twenty knots snorting down our necks we lunge for Ambrosia Beach.
Tomorrow the Brooks Peninsula brooding under its cap.
For now, a sweet shore.
Silence.

Cape Cook

Whee-ha!
We hurtle past the cape.
Fifteen-knot winds and a following tide.
The kelp is a slippery highway with its fronds aligned in our favour.
We are strange stick creatures scrabbling along the surface.
A seagull hovers in the wind.
Dips its beak for a taste.

McLean Island

For every beach a bear.
Everybody needs to make a living!
But not just now—today this beach belongs to us!
The men get macho, hollering, thumping chests, throwing rocks.
When that doesn't work they thrash the bushes with sticks.
Finally the bear wanders off—we're safe for the night.
In the morning, fresh cougar tracks in camp.

Grassy Island

Squished playdough worms.
Surely a child formed these rocks!
Only a five-year-old would colour black and orange oystercatchers.
A crayoned sun and the orange rays of the sunstar.
How can I believe these fossils are ancient?
I'm feeling sort of young myself.
And foolish.

Kapoose Creek

A long, long morning walk for water.
Fresh cougar tracks tell a story of pivot and spring.
The August fog won't lift—we stand around and wait and wait.
An invisible raven says a word as we launch into the abyss.
We read the chart by ear: gravel, boomer, reef.
Sometimes a sharp command: Hard right!
Adrenaline surges us past the danger.

Tatchu Point

A kelp bed.
An otter nursery.
Soft mewling baby cries.
Each kelp head has tasselled ears.
The waves waggle them up and down.
A sea lion rises up off John's stern, a looming black monster.
It slips back under without a sound.

Little Espinosa Inlet

So much traffic!
Teens roaring around.
Speedboats stuffed with fishing gear.
A family out for an afternoon in the canoe.
Water taxis ferrying less hardy kayakers home.
We race slowly for the take-out point.
Last one to get there wins.

Note

"And See What Happens," "Frog River" and "Last One to Get There" were all published in slightly different form as chapbooks.

Gratitudes

Nunsulsailus, Chris Paul, my crewmates. The Ladies Who Cook: Henny Hagedorn, Carol Grant, Joanne Dunn and Joy Hill. John Grant and the RCMP—thanks for trusting me with a paddle. Ed Hill for help with photographs. Earl Moulton, too. John Kimantas and Angus Weller for advice with maps. Marianne and Urs Schildknecht of Northern Rockies Lodge in Muncho Lake for the hospitality and the gift of the flight to Frog River and the stay in the cabin. Lyn Hancock, Liz Strachan and Mary Cox, who were there too. Nanaimo Paddlers for all the water that's flowed under my kayak. The Nanaimo Women Poets for good readings and good poetry over the years. Kathy and Kath, who never doubted. Mario and Jess for letting me go. Gordon for being there when I got home. David Payne for just about everything.

I am grateful too, to all the teachers I met on the Vision Quest journey. I will never forget your words. Thanks especially to John Elliott, Ken Innes, George Innes, William Wasden, Rita Robertson, Esther Shackelly, Leslie Marrion, Cecil Hill, Cecil Johnson, Elaine Assu Price. To the Hartley Bay elder who said "Our canoe has overturned" and to the Qualicum elder who mentioned paddling backward, thank you. I am sorry I was unable, after much searching, to find your names.

Thanks to Joe Denham for throwing me in the deep end. The poems are the better for it.

Finally, thanks to Roy Vickers, who taught me the most important thing of all: "Don't be scared."

About the Author

Ursula Vaira grew up in northern BC; after studying Education at UBC, she taught school on the northern coast and in the Arctic, then moved to Vancouver Island in the early eighties. She worked at Oolichan Books for ten years, then founded Leaf Press in 2001. Ursula loves wilderness camping and kayaking, and has a passion for the west coast—in the summer of 2005, she kayaked with a group from Port Hardy to Zeballos, around Cape Scott and Cape Cook. In 1997 she paddled by Coast Salish canoe from Hazelton to Victoria as part of Roy Henry Vickers's Vision Quest to raise addictions awareness and funds to build an all-nations recovery centre on Vancouver Island. Through these and other experiences she has learned the power of the arduous journey as a metaphor for personal growth. In truth, all journeys lead to the interior.

Her poems have appeared in literary journals and anthologies published by Hawthorne Society, Outlaw Editions, Anvil Press, Quills, and the B.C. Federation of Writers. The title poem of this collection, "And See What Happens," was a finalist in the CBC Literary Competition and was published in slightly different form as a chapbook called *A Thousand Miles*. "Last One to Get There" was published in a chapbook titled *Little Espinoza*, and "Frog River" formed a chapbook of the same title.

More poetry from Caitlin Press

Beautiful Mutants, Adam Pottle
104 pp, pb, ISBN 978-1-894759-59-5

Adam Pottle cracks open the world of disability, illuminating it with an idiom that is both unsettling and exhilarating. Difficult as their circumstances may seem, Pottle's denizens learn to navigate the world with creative resolve, even defiance, searching for an identity that includes their disabilities rather than spites them. His poems scrape our nerves; they test and undermine poetic forms, challenging our own sensibilities in the process.

Unfurled: Collected Poetry from Northern BC Women, Debbie Keahey
208 pp, pb, ISBN 978-1-894759-52-6, $22.95

Ambulance lights flash as a baby is born on a busy city street, pine beetles paint forests a palette of new colours, a young boy faces a watery death under the ice of a frozen lake, and a mother stands in a bathtub at midnight wearing only her gumboots. In this anthology, poets share their refreshing, intriguing, mystical and sometimes mythical insights into rural and urban life.

Walk Myself Home: An Anthology to End Violence Against Women, Andrea Routley
184 pp, pb, ISBN 978-1-894759-51-9, $22.95

There is an epidemic of violence against women in Canada and the world. For many women physical and sexual assault, or the threat of such violence, is a daily reality. *Walk Myself Home* is an anthology of poetry, fiction, nonfiction and oral interviews on the subject of violence against women including contributions by Kate Braid, Yasuko Thahn and Susan Musgrave.